Making Love Last a Lifetime

ADAM HAMILTON

Making Love Last a Lifetime

BIBLICAL PERSPECTIVES ON LOVE, MARRIAGE, AND SEX

ABINGDON PRESS
Nashville

Making Love Last a Lifetime:
Biblical Perspectives on Love, Marriage, and Sex

Copyright © 2004 by Abingdon Press.

This book is printed on acid-free, elemental chlorine-free paper.

ISBN 0-687-00726-7
ISBN 0-687-06184-9

04 05 06 07 08 09 10 11 12 13—10 9 8 7 6 5 4 3 2 1
Manufactured in the United States of America.

To LaVon

ACKNOWLEDGMENTS

This book would not have been possible without the people of the Church of the Resurrection and their willingness to share their struggles and joys in the areas of love, marriage, and sex. I am particularly indebted to those couples who met with me one-on-one to share their stories.

I would be remiss in not pausing to acknowledge the important role my assistant plays both in my ministry and in the writing of books and sermons. Sue Thompson's ministry makes what I do possible. For this book she organized teams of people to sort and analyze the information from our surveys, and she served as my research partner and sounding board as I prepared this material.

I am grateful to the team of wonderful people who are a part of the worship planning process at the Church of the Resurrection. Our pastors and staff help shape my analysis and understanding of these issues. They are a remarkable group of people. For those using this book in a small-group study, it is important to note that the video materials for this series would not have been possible without the incredible work of Connie Stella and her team in Saving Grace Productions—the video ministry of our church.

Finally, I want to express appreciation to my wife, LaVon, for being willing to share the most personal and intimate parts of our life together in the hope of encouraging others. Most of what I have learned about love, marriage, and sex, I have learned from her.

CONTENTS

Chapter 1
Venus and Mars in the Beginning 11

Chapter 2
What Women Wish Men Knew About Women 25

Chapter 3
What Men Wish Women Knew About Men 39

Chapter 4
After the Honeymoon Is Over 53

Chapter 5
The Habits of Unhealthy Marriages 67

Chapter 6
God's Plan for Sexual Intimacy 83

Chapter 7
The Ministry and Meaning of Faithfulness 99

Chapter 8
Making Love Last a Lifetime 115

CHAPTER 1

Venus and Mars in the Beginning

Then the LORD God said, "It is not good that the man should be alone; I will make him a helper as his partner."... So the LORD God caused a deep sleep to fall upon the man, and he slept; then he took one of his ribs and closed up its place with flesh. And the rib that the LORD God had taken from the man he made into a woman and brought her to the man. Then the man said,

"This at last is bone of my bones
and flesh of my flesh;
this one shall be called Woman,
for out of Man this one was taken."

Therefore a man leaves his father and his mother and clings to his wife, and they become one flesh. And the man and his wife were both naked, and were not ashamed.

(Genesis 2:18, 21-25)

June 5, 1982—this was the day my wife, LaVon, and I were married. It was one week after my high school graduation. We had had one session of premarital counseling. We both came from households that had experienced divorce. We definitely were not prepared for marriage.

I recall one family member announcing to me the day before the wedding that our marriage "would never last," and I remember having the sinking feeling that perhaps this person was right.

Following our wedding, LaVon and I loaded up a rental trailer with our "garage sale" furniture and wedding presents and moved five hours away to begin college and our new life together. On the way the muffler fell off the car—it felt a bit like an omen. Since we had a total of $200 in our bank account, that mishap was particularly disconcerting! Later that day we unloaded the trailer and settled into our little apartment with mixed feelings of excitement and fear.

In the years since, LaVon and I have had our ups and downs—times of falling in and falling out of love. We have faced temptations, tragedies, and challenges to our marriage. And we have grown up; we are not the same people we were in 1982. But through the years, and despite the challenges, our love has grown deeper than we ever imagined. It is, after our faith, the richest part of our lives.

My aim in writing this book is to help you discover some of the keys to developing a healthy, satisfying, and successful marriage. I will draw upon insights gleaned from surveys of over two thousand single and married persons in my congregation; experiences shared by couples I interviewed in preparation for this book, including a very special group of people who have been married for more than fifty years; and reflections based upon fifteen years of counseling individuals and couples. I will incorporate some of the insights from excellent books by others who have written on the subject. I will also share some of my own personal experiences in marriage. But finally, and most importantly, in each chapter I will lift up insights from the Bible and resources from the Christian faith that are both practical and helpful as you seek to make love last a lifetime.

I have written this book not only for married couples but also for singles who anticipate being married at some time in their lives. If you are single, this book can equip and prepare you to have a successful relationship. If you are married, this book is aimed at helping you grow in your relationship with your spouse so that you can experience all that God intends marriage to be.

Love, marriage, and sex are issues that are important to God, as evidenced by the fact that the Bible has so much to say about them. One of the first stories in the Bible is about marriage and the relationship between a man and a woman—a story we will examine in this chapter. Throughout the Law of Moses, issues of marriage and sexuality come up again and again. One entire book of the Bible is devoted to romantic love: The Song of Solomon, also known as The Song of Songs. The prophets and the writers of Proverbs address the topics of love, marriage, and sex on numerous occasions.

Jesus performs his first miracle at a wedding, likens himself to a bridegroom, uses marriage as the theme of a parable, and offers a wide variety of teachings that are directly applicable to marriage. The apostle Paul calls marriage a "mystery" that portrays the love of Christ for the church. Paul frequently addresses issues of how men and women are meant to relate to each other, and he even writes frankly about matters of sexual intimacy within marriage. Throughout Scripture, God's relationship first with Israel and then with the church is likened to a husband's relationship with his bride.

It is not only appropriate, it is incumbent upon the church to address these issues. The Bible has answers to our questions about healthy and lasting relationships. We need to get that message out! If the church is not doing its job in teaching about love, marriage, and sex, where will people go to learn about these things? Television? Hollywood? Romance novels? Women's and men's magazines? The church's silence on these issues is at least in part to blame for the state of marriage in our society. Divorce continues to be a likely prospect for many who marry; and, among those who do not get divorced, many fail to experience the joy God intended people to have in marriage.

Finally, an underlying premise of this book is that love, marriage, and sex are all God's idea. God designed us and designed these things as gifts to us. Only in exploring biblical perspectives on these issues can we hope to experience the blessings that these three gifts—love, marriage, and sex—are meant to hold for us. God created us to have successful relationships with others, and the Scriptures offer us guidance regarding God's plan for this part of our lives.

As we begin this journey together, we will seek to learn all that we can about relationships between men and women. We will have the benefit of learning from others, exploring research, and analyzing the results of nearly 2,500 surveys filled out and returned by men and women in my congregation. In addition, I encourage you to open your Bible and listen for its truths. Read for yourself the passages of Scripture listed at the beginning of the chapters in this book and meditate on what they say to you. Carefully read and reflect on the questions and suggestions at the end of each chapter. Whether you are a deeply committed Christian or just someone who wants to have better relationships, this study could mark the beginning of discoveries that could change your life.

Why Is Marriage So Hard?

Let's begin by recognizing that having a successful relationship with a member of the opposite sex is not easy! The Centers for Disease Control and Prevention and the National Center for Health Statistics recently released divorce statistics based upon a national study of 10,847 women. The study revealed that 43 percent of all marriages end in separation or divorce within the first 15 years.[1] Another sign of the challenge of building a successful relationship is the age at which people are marrying, which has risen dramatically in the last decade.[2] In addition, the number of persons living together outside marriage rose by 72 percent in the 1990s,[3] indicative, in many cases, of the fear of committing to marriage without trying things out first.

Clearly there is a challenge to making love last a lifetime. One of the factors in this struggle is that men and women are quite different. We see the world differently, hear things differently, and approach life differently.

Not long ago I conducted a lighthearted and informal survey of my staff. I e-mailed them and invited the women to tell me about their frustrations with men, and I invited the men to tell me about their frustrations with women. Soon the e-mails were flying into my office. Here is a bit of what the women said:

The Top 10 Things Men Do That Frustrate Women

10. Men think they know everything and treat women as if they don't know anything.
9. Sports!

15

8. Men lack creativity when buying gifts; they need to be given hints, and then they don't get the hints!
7. Men never clean up after themselves.
6. Men don't follow instructions.
5. Men are always "ready for action."
4. Men don't notice when things need to be done.
3. Men can never find anything, even when it's right in front of their face.
2. Men belch and then smile as if it were a great treat for all those around them.

And the number-one thing these women said was frustrating about men:

1. MEN DON'T LISTEN!!!

Now, there are men among my staff; but most of them refused to respond—which may have had something to do with men's inability to follow instructions, as noted above! While I had seventy responses from women, I had only sixteen from men. One man wrote, "Nothing frustrates me about women," but then he went on to list several things that would frustrate him if anything did frustrate him! Here is a summary of the men's responses:

The Top 10 Things Women Do That Frustrate Men

10. Women need to talk about everything!
9. Women think they know what you're thinking.
8. Women think you should know what they're thinking!
7. Women focus on the minutia and miss the big picture.
6. Shoes!

5. Women are utterly indecisive.
4. Women are terrible drivers.
3. Women say, "This sale saved us so much money," when, had there not been a sale, they wouldn't have spent any money!
2. Gossip, gossip, gossip.

And the number-one thing about women that drives men crazy:

1. The assumptions and stereotypes women have about men.

Of course, most of the men were careful to say that none of these things was true of their own wives or significant others!

Although my survey was in no way definitive, it clearly indicated that both men and women have their issues. These issues arise from the fact that God created us to be very different from each other, and not just anatomically. Our brains are different. Our biochemistry is different. Our ways of seeing the world are different. The title of John Gray's best-selling book expresses it well: *Men Are From Mars, Women Are From Venus.*

Learning how to cope with and appreciate these differences goes a long way toward improving relationships. But there is one other reality that exacerbates the problems raised by our differences: our human condition.

By nature we desperately want to be loved and to be in relationship with others; but we also struggle with our own selfishness, self-centeredness, pettiness, and hardheartedness. We struggle with temptation, and we wrestle with our own desires. These are spiritual issues, and they are common to us all.

That is why we cannot have the very best in our marriages or relationships without including spiritual perspectives. We need the wisdom of God as found in the Bible. So, as we begin our study, let's turn to the biblical account of the very first wedding, the story of Adam and Eve as told beginning in the second chapter of Genesis.

A Brief Look at God's Big Idea

We discover in Genesis that God has created the first human being, in the form of a man. The story of Creation is told in a wonderful, simple, childlike way. God creates the man and places him in the midst of paradise, providing for him all the most wonderful things to eat and drink and the most amazing things to see. God is even personally present to Adam.

Yet God, watching this human being over time, notices that the man has a need that even God cannot fulfill. The man is alone. So, the story goes, God creates all the beasts of the field and the birds of the air. But even though the garden is now filled with creatures and activity and noise, the man is still alone, the only one of his kind. So God determines to make for him a companion and helper so he will not be alone.

Now, God could do that simply by replicating the man. Certainly God could devise some form of nonsexual reproduction for populating the world with people. But can you imagine a world inhabited only by men? There would be no minds to read. We would all speak in grunts and incomplete sentences. There would be bratwursts and burgers and beer, baseball and basketball and football all year long. The concept of making one's bed would be unheard of. And we would have disposable clothes—wear them until they stand up by themselves and then throw them away!

But God decides that is not such a good idea. Instead, God determines that the man needs a woman, a creature very much the same as man and yet mysteriously, maddeningly, wonderfully different. So God creates the new and improved model of the human being: a woman! When God brings the woman to him, the man says, "This at last is what I've been longing for; she is flesh of my flesh and bone of my bone." Then the two embrace and become one flesh, and marriage is born. And they are naked, but there is no shame in this.

Now let's examine the four key lessons that this story has to offer us about the relationship between men and women, lessons we will study in more detail in future chapters.

1. *God* created men and women to be different. *God* designed those differences. As such they are a gift, not a curse. They are to be valued and understood, not hated and despised. Somehow our differences are essential to God's plan.

2. Men and women *need* each other. I do not mean that we all need to be married. In fact, the New Testament says that the highest calling and the preferred lifestyle for a Christian is singleness in which one is free to devote one's whole life and time to service for Christ. But even in singleness we need the opposite sex. We need friendships with members of the opposite sex. We need their help. We need the uniqueness and giftedness of the opposite sex. That is why, in my denomination, we welcome male and female pastors—because in the

pastoral ministry, as elsewhere, we are incomplete until both men and women are represented. It is also the reason we need more women in politics and business and why we are blessed when men go into the fields of nursing and education alongside women.

3. Sex and sexuality were meant to be beautiful. They were designed by God as a good part of creation. We see this in the last line of our Scripture passage: "And the man and his wife were both naked, and were not ashamed."

4. Finally, and most importantly, note that the union of a man and woman—marriage—was designed by God as the solution to a problem. The problem was that the first human was alone and needed companionship, and he was unable to live as God intended without a partner. God designed Adam and Eve to be helpers and companions for each other ... which leads us to the most important point for you to remember, and the basic idea behind this book.

Marriage Is a Calling From God

One deep, spiritual truth on this topic is so important that it cannot be overemphasized. In fact, it forms the premise of this entire book: Marriage is a *calling* from God. God designed marriage as a way of meeting the basic needs of human beings—needs for companionship and help. The basic orientation of marriage is serving, giving, and sacrificing.

Choosing to marry is choosing to answer a calling from God toward the person you are marrying, although you may not always feel like answering that call. To the degree that you remain focused on this mission, you will find joy and meaning in your marriage, even when things are not perfect.

I felt a calling from God to be a pastor. I studied, prepared, and finally was ordained by my bishop. There are days when I get frustrated with my job. There are times I do not enjoy it (not many, but a few). I have had thoughts, on occasion, about doing something else. But then I remember my calling; it was God who called me to this work. This was part of God's purpose for my life. My ministry is an act of faithfulness and obedience to God.

And so it is with marriage. Marriage is not simply the next step after falling in love. Marriage is serious business. It is a calling from God—a lifelong mission of service and caring and ministry to another human being—seeking to be, on God's behalf, a companion and helper to another.

When I married LaVon, I accepted God's call to love her, minister to her, and care for her in Christ's name until that day when God calls her, or me, to heaven. There are times when pursuing this calling is rich and rewarding. There are other times when for one or the other of us this calling is maddening, frustrating, and challenging. It is at those times in particular that it is helpful for us to remember that marriage is a calling, a mission from God.

Throughout this book, I will be sharing information with you about marriage, about the Scriptures, about relationships. But information alone is not enough. You need to play your part. I encourage you to make the effort to strengthen those relationships that are most meaningful to you. Ask God to help. You cannot do it alone.

Great marriages do not just happen; they require discipline, sacrifice, and effort. The best marriages are found only when we discover God's purposes, plans, and principles as they relate to the relationship between a man and a woman. It is the discovery of these ideas that opens the door to the kind of love that lasts a lifetime.

---

[1] See http://www.cdc.gov/nchs/releases/01news/firstmarr.htm
[2] US Census Bureau; see http://www.census.gov
[3] See http://latimes.com/news/nationworld/nation/la-082001cohab-it.story

Personal Reflection

Individuals

- Read one-to-two chapters of the Song of Solomon each day this week, asking yourself the following questions: What are the various characters feeling in this chapter? What do they do that fosters their love? How can we learn from their example?
- Find one or more ways to affirm and celebrate the differences of your spouse—or, if single, someone special of the opposite sex—(for example, do something he or she likes to do; look for the positive side of something you ordinarily consider negative or irritating; offer genuine praise for one of his or her differences; and so forth).
- List all the reasons you need and appreciate your spouse—or, if single, someone special of the opposite sex. Give thanks to God for these gifts *each day this week.*

Couples

- Talk together about those irritations that can build up, leading to resentment and conflict. Agree up front to speak the truth in love and listen to each other without debating or becoming defensive. Commit to pray about these things throughout the week, asking God to change your hearts and attitudes. End by sharing the lists you compiled of the reasons you need and appreciate each other.

CHAPTER 2

What Women Wish Men Knew About Women

Husbands, love your wives, just as Christ loved the church and gave himself up for her.

(Ephesians 5:25)

As God's chosen ones, holy and beloved, clothe yourselves with compassion, kindness, humility, meekness, and patience. Bear with one another and, if anyone has a complaint against another, forgive each other; just as the Lord has forgiven you, so you also must forgive. Above all, clothe yourselves with love, which binds everything together in perfect harmony. And let the peace of Christ rule in your hearts, to which indeed you were called in the one body. And be thankful. Let the word of Christ dwell in you richly; teach and admonish one another in all wisdom; and with gratitude in your hearts sing psalms, hymns, and spiritual songs to God. And whatever you do, in word or deed, do everything in the name of the Lord Jesus, giving thanks to God the Father through him.

(Colossians 3:12-17)

How do you meet the needs of your spouse? That is a million-dollar question. My firm belief is that the Bible can provide some valuable insights into this challenge, which all married couples face. Since God did not create us with the ability to read minds, it is up to us to learn as much as we can about the opposite sex. That is the subject of the next two chapters.

As we continue our examination of God's big idea behind love, marriage, and sex, let's review what we have learned so far:

• Men and women are very different.
• Those differences, coupled with our human condition—our own failures, shortcomings, and sin—make it challenging to have a successful relationship or marriage.
• God designed our differences so that men and women might complement one another, help one another, and meet one another's needs.
• Marriage is a calling from God, a mission in which each partner seeks to minister to and meet certain needs of the other. It is this last idea that will serve as a springboard for the next two chapters.

One of the keys to a successful marriage is paying attention to your partner. It is only when you know the needs of your spouse that you can meet those needs. My goal in this chapter is to help men understand women's needs. If you are a woman reading this, see if you agree with these observations. (We will try to help women understand men's needs in the next chapter.)

Men, what I am about to share with you is not something I read in a book; nor is it something I learned in a seminary class. The women of my congregation gave this information to me—1,000 married women and 500 single women who filled out a questionnaire on love, marriage, and sex. We are going to examine what women said in response to the question, "What do men do that makes you feel loved?"

But first, allow me to offer a metaphor that might help you understand the importance of seeking to meet a woman's needs.

A Love Bank

Both Dr. Willard Harley and Dr. Barbara DeAngelis have written numerous books on marriage, based on their work with thousands of couples. Both authors use a helpful metaphor to describe a woman's heart. They speak of it as a "love bank." They note that in a relationship, actions on the part of both partners constitute deposits to and withdrawals from the woman's love bank.

When a husband demonstrates love for his wife in certain ways, deposits are made to her love bank. When a wife takes care of the home or the children, when she gives herself to the husband emotionally or physically, withdrawals take place. Thus, a relationship is characterized by ongoing deposits and withdrawals.

Guys, when you first marry, there tends to be a huge balance in your wife's love bank. You have romanced her. You have stayed up for hours talking to her on the phone. You have spent lots of quality time with her. You have told her how beautiful she is, bought her a ring, and whisked her off on a honeymoon.

But then the honeymoon ends, and life settles into a comfortable pattern. And you settle into making regular withdrawals from the love bank. Unfortunately, you are no longer making hefty deposits into the account. In fact, sometimes days or even weeks may go by between deposits. That huge balance begins to be whittled away. But you do not know it because you do not keep track of your wife's love account as closely as you keep track of your bank account.

Our wives can operate with a deficit in this account for long periods of time. The only overdraft warnings we get are in the form of short temper, irritation, coldness to our physical advances, or tears. Sometimes when our wives try to tell us we are overdrawn, we become defensive or angry and do not hear what they are saying—and we become even more overdrawn.

When a woman's love bank operates in overdraft mode for a long period of time, it will eventually go bankrupt and the account will be closed. She will have nothing left to give. In marriages, many times this status is formalized when the wife files for divorce.

What complicates things even further is that there are times when we try to make deposits, certain that we are doing something just for her, only to find that her love bank operates on an entirely different kind of currency. We do not understand why buying kitchen appliances or a new lawn mower or that lacy bit of string from a lingerie shop did not count as a deposit to her account.

Thus it is critical that you understand what constitutes a deposit in the love bank and that you regularly put more into the account than you are taking out. This is one of the keys to a woman having a marriage that is emotionally fulfilling for her. What I am about to share with you are the top four things that the women in my congregation said constituted deposits in their love banks; that is, what women most frequently cited as making them feel closest to their husbands.

What Married Women Want

It is no secret that there is often a wide gap between the desires of men and women. We are made differently, and so our needs are different. It is all a part of God's plan, so that we complement and complete each other. Because of these differences, living together as husband and wife takes some adjusting, listening, and just plain work in order for both partners to remain satisfied and even joyful about the relationship. Let's take a look at the items on the "wish lists" of the married women in my congregation:

Demonstrations of Affection

Wives indicated that they feel loved when their husbands touch them in intimate but nonsexual ways. Women feel loved when we men hold them, hug them, kiss them, and cuddle with them. They enjoy back rubs and foot rubs and tender touches. But this touching means the most to them when it is done as an expression of our love and our desire to bless them, not as a way of meeting our own needs or as a precursor to another form of physical intimacy. They are not against the latter, but they crave the former: acts of affection and touch for its own sake.

Married women reported that they appreciate not only physical acts of affection but also words. Over and over they indicated how much it means to hear "I love you" on a regular basis. Those who had been married more than forty years frequently cited this as a regular part of their relationship—in fact, they said that it was the part of the relationship that allowed their marriage to succeed.

Wives stated that they also enjoy special surprises from their husbands or other unexpected ways of expressing affection, and the women who had been married the longest gave the most specific examples. Women in their seventies noted that they feel loved when their husbands write poetry for them, bring them coffee in the morning, or surprise them with other small but meaningful gifts.

So, on our list of things that women want from men, the item at the top is demonstrations of affection. That is not too difficult is it, guys? Think back to when you were dating, and bring back some of the little things you used to do to show your love. While you are at it, use your creativity to come up with some new ones.

Demonstrations of Attentiveness

The second item on the list of things that women want from men is for us to give them our undivided attention. This does not mean listening to them while the television is on or while we are reading the newspaper. It means taking the time to listen without interruptions, to demonstrate that we value what they have to say. When we stop, look at them, and ask questions about their thoughts or feelings, they feel loved.

One woman wrote, "I wish my husband knew how important it is to stop and look into my eyes and just to tell me I am important to him." Wives repeatedly noted that they feel most distant when their husbands fail to listen and treat them as though their feelings and thoughts do not matter. This is deadly to a relationship. To paraphrase an old saying, sometimes the way to a woman's heart is through our ears.

I once heard that the average woman has the need to speak thousands more words per day than the average man. In other words, when the average man gets home from work, he has already used up his allotment of words, while the woman is just getting warmed up!

Our survey indicated that women not only want us to listen and value their thoughts and words, they also want to know what is going on inside our heads. They report that this knowledge produces feelings of intimacy for them. Women feel closest to us when we share our thoughts, dreams, and ideas. They long for us to be vulnerable and to open up to them.

The problem, of course, is that most men have had years of training to do just the opposite. From the time we were in preschool, we were taught that "big boys don't cry" and that it is dangerous to show our vulnerable side. We have learned to process things without talking or sharing our feelings. Yet these same habits, which in some settings have proven useful, can damage or even destroy our relationships with women.

Guys, I encourage you to make an effort to be attentive to your wife. Work on showing your vulnerable side. Make listening a priority just for a week, and see if it does not make a difference. Communication is a key to a happy and lasting marriage. Sharing is a great way of showing you care, and it can revitalize your relationship.

Active Involvement With the Children and Home

A third need that married women expressed—and a way in which men will make either deposits or withdrawals—is for us to be involved in activities at home. We were created by God to help one another, and women noted that they need our help. Women ages thirty to fifty said they feel especially loved when we take time to be involved with our children or, later, our grandchildren.

Many women are nurturers, and one of the activities they appreciate most is when we notice things that need to be done around the house and then take the initiative to do our part. Often this involves helping with children; but it may also include helping with the car, with home repairs, or with cleaning. This concern for family matters and things around the home seems to be very real.

Demonstrations of Appreciation

Finally, the married women in the survey said they long to be appreciated. Like any of us, they want to feel that we notice what they do for us. They want to be cherished, treasured, and not taken for granted. Conversely, a number of wives indicated that they feel most distant when their husbands are critical, negative, or unappreciative.

In a long-term relationship it is easy to take our mates for granted, to see only the negative in them, or to overlook all that they do that is right. One of the exercises I recommend for husbands is to stop and spend fifteen minutes thanking God for all the blessings their wives bring them. I encourage husbands to write notes to their wives, letting them know how much they are appreciated.

But the real challenge is to make this behavior a part of daily life.

Dr. Barbara DeAngelis' book *What Women Want Men to Know* summarizes what women most want and need from their husbands. She notes that the way to make deposits into a woman's love bank is to provide her with the three A's on a regular basis: attention, affection, and appreciation. Based on our survey, I would add a fourth: active involvement with the children and home.

What Wives Would Change About Their Husbands

In the survey, married women were also asked what they would change about their husbands. Interestingly enough, the item that came up most frequently was wanting their husbands to be more actively involved in their faith. This wish, expressed across all age groups, showed a deep longing on the part of wives to share a spiritual journey with their husbands. Some of the other wishes listed were that husbands be more positive, less critical, better organized, and that they take better care of their bodies.

One fascinating tidbit: By age fifty, the second-most frequently given answer to the question of what they would change was "nothing." And by the sixties and seventies, that answer was the most frequently given. We could speculate about the reasons; but I thought it was best expressed by one woman in my congregation, who said, "We've been married more than forty years now, and I've finally got him just about the way I like him!"

It is my hope and prayer that men begin to take the needs of women more seriously. Perhaps thoughtful consideration of the ideas above will be a first step. Men, I believe that if you focus on pleasing your wife, you will also enjoy the benefits of a renewed and invigorated relationship.

The love you give to your wife will return to you. It is worth the effort!

What Single Women Want

Now that we have discussed what married women want, I am guessing that there are single men reading this book who might be interested in knowing what single women want.

Based on our survey, here are the top five characteristics that single women look for as they consider entering into a relationship with a man. The list changes very little as women age.

1. Strong Christian faith   75%
2. Honesty/character   45%
3. Sense of humor   40%
4. Caring/loving/kind   40%
5. Respectful   30%

You may be wondering whether physical appearance was on the list. It was for single women in their twenties. But among single women in their thirties, only fifteen percent listed appearance; yet the number who noted that they were looking for a man who was Christian had almost doubled. Apparently most single women believe that attractiveness is more a function of a man's heart than his "abs."

Finally, single women were asked what they find unattractive in a man. Here, both married and single men would do well to pay attention. Nearly every woman who was single said she is turned off by men who are self-centered, arrogant, or egotistical.

Connecting the Survey to the Scriptures

The apostle Paul wrote, "Husbands, love your wives as Christ loved the church" (Ephesians 5:25). This scriptural command once again illustrates the Bible's ability to offer us wisdom that is precisely what we need; for in fulfilling this verse and others like it, we find that our marriages begin to soar.

How did Christ love the church? Think about it. Even before there was a church, when it was just an idea in his mind, Jesus Christ was laying down his life for us. Jesus' death on the cross was the ultimate demonstration of God's love for us. Christ took upon himself our burdens. He gave everything he had to serve us, love us, and save us.

The word describing this kind of love in Scripture is a Greek word many of you are familiar with: *agape*. Agape is defined as "spontaneous self-giving love expressed freely without calculation of cost or gain to the giver or merit on the part of the receiver."

Husbands, this is our calling: to bless, encourage, minister to, and love sacrificially. Marriage is meant to be a gift from God. Our wives long to be treasured today just as much as when we first walked with them down the aisle. And part of our calling is to envelope them in this kind of self-giving love.

How can we do this? In my congregation, the women tell us that we express agape

- when we demonstrate affection to them through touch, words, and small acts of kindness;
- when we pay attention to them by listening, valuing their thoughts, noticing what is important to them, inviting them to share their feelings, and sharing our innermost thoughts with them;
- when we are genuinely engaged in the home and family, helping our wives and loving our children;
- when we express appreciation and gratitude for who they are and what they have done rather than taking them for granted or criticizing them.

Above all, do not forget one of the most important findings of our survey: Women have a deep longing for us to be partners in faith with them. They have a dream that we might actually pray with them, worship with them, grow in faith with them. They know that we will never be the husbands we could be until we have invited Christ into our lives. They long to share that part of their lives with us.

Men, if you are not yet ready to consider becoming a Christian, then allow me to offer one word of advice: Do not mock your wife's faith. When you do, you make a huge withdrawal from her love bank because you devalue the one thing that is most important to her. Do not be threatened by the fact that her faith in God takes precedence over her love for you. In fact, your wife's faith in Christ empowers her to love you even more, to bless you, and to become the kind of loving partner you have always dreamed of.

In the words of the apostle Paul, "Husbands, love your wives, as Christ loved the church" (Ephesians 5:25). That advice is your key to making love last a lifetime. It is also what women want men to know most of all, that sacrificial love, agape, binds a man to a woman. And it makes them one with God.

Personal Reflection

Individuals
- Look over the list of what makes women feel loved. Women: Which of these are you most in need of? Men: Which of these do you need to work on?
- Men only: Read 1 Corinthians 13:1-8a. Insert your name in the place of "love" and "it" in verses 4-7 to see how you measure up to God's desires.
- Men only: In Proverbs 31:10-31, we see a husband expressing gratitude for his wife. Pray a prayer of thanksgiving for the woman you love. Then write a Proverbs 31 letter for her—a poem or note thanking her for all she has done for you. Praise, affirm, and encourage her. Take your wife on a date and give this poem or note to her (See below.).
- Husbands only: Read Ephesians 5:25. What are the practical implications of this verse for your marriage?

Couples
- Discuss your responses to the first bulleted point above. Men: Ask, "What can I do for you to bless and encourage you? When do you feel closest to me? Are there things I do that push you away?"
- Men: Plan a date for this week. If a traditional night out is not possible, consider having a lunch date or a late-night "at-home" date. Remember to share your letter.

CHAPTER 3

What Men Wish Women Knew About Men

Be subject to one another out of reverence for Christ.

Wives, be subject to your husbands as you are to the Lord. For the husband is the head of the wife just as Christ is the head of the church, the body of which he is the Savior. Just as the church is subject to Christ, so also wives ought to be, in every-thing, to their husbands. . . .

Each of you [husbands], however, should love his wife as himself, and a wife should respect her husband.
(Ephesians 5:21-24, 33)

In the previous chapter, we looked at some things women wish men knew about women. Now it is time to examine the other side of the coin and look at things from a man's point of view.

God created men and women to be very different, with different needs; and that is good. Aside from the need for sports and power tools, men also need women. Women complement men's gifts and compensate for their weak-nesses. Men need women.

As we begin this look into the needs of men, let's review what we have learned so far about women. We have tried to help men understand four of the most commonly mentioned desires women have concerning their relationships with men. These desires are affection, attention, active involvement in the home, and appreciation. We learned that the Scriptures call husbands to love their wives with a form of love the New Testament calls *agape*—sacrificial love, the kind of love that Jesus Christ demonstrated in laying down his life for us.

We also introduced an important metaphor to help men understand the needs of their mates and the importance of meeting those needs. Willard Harley, Barbara DeAngelis, and others have popularized the idea of the "love bank." They note that in some ways, women's hearts are like banks, giving out love or taking in love on deposit. One of the important elements of a successful marriage is maintaining a healthy balance in our mates' love banks.

What Married Men Want

Now that we have examined the love currency of women, let's draw on this imagery of a love bank, apply it to men, and seek to understand what constitutes a deposit in a man's love bank. To help in this task, the men in my congregation were asked, "What is it that a woman does that makes you feel loved?" Nearly 1,000 men responded to the survey; 150 of them were single, and the rest were married. Let's take a look at the responses most frequently given by the married men.

Admiration

Married men in all the age groups up to but not including the seventies mentioned somewhere on their list that they feel most loved when their wives admire them; take pride in them; or otherwise demonstrate support, verbal encouragement, or belief in them. For men in their twenties and thirties, this item was ranked first.

Author Gary Chapman, in his book *The Five Love Languages,* calls this the "words of affirmation" love language.[1] Women sometimes speak in a derogatory way about the "fragile male ego," but I wonder if that is really helpful. Perhaps instead we should acknowledge that God has designed the male psyche to include a need to provide for, care for, and impress a woman. Throughout nature we find this principle at work: Males try to win the hearts of females by demonstrating their colors, their spirit, their fight. Most of us men want to be some woman's hero, so that she will admire us or be proud of us. God designed men that way.

Listening and Sharing

Married men in nearly every age category of our survey indicated that another time they feel most loved is when their wives listen to them and encourage them to share important things. I found this astounding, considering the fact that in our survey the married women in this congregation said they wanted their husbands to talk more!

I was perplexed by this discrepancy until one day, driving in my car, I heard on the radio Toby Keith's song "I Wanna Talk About Me!" I laughed so hard I almost had to stop the car; but when I stopped laughing, it occurred to me that the lyrics may have provided the explanation I had been looking for. Men want to talk; but they need time, space, and an invitation to share things that are important to them.

One of the things I value most about my wife, LaVon, is the way she listens and celebrates when I achieve some victory or success. I do not feel comfortable calling my friends and telling them about successes at church because it would come across as bragging. But LaVon and I are able to celebrate these things together. She asks to hear about them and then gets excited for me. Of course, most men do not want or need to talk as much as some women do; but we do enjoy sharing things that we are proud of with our wives and having them get excited with us.

Family Support

Married men in the survey from their forties on indicated that one of the times they feel most loved is when their wives care for their physical and emotional needs and the physical and emotional needs of their children. Willard Harley talks about this as "domestic support."[2] Gary Chapman calls it the "acts of service" love language.[3]

As a man who grew up in the 1960s and 70s, I am a bit embarrassed by this concept, having been reared to believe that the concept of domestic support—that women are to take care of children, husband, and home—is somehow a sexist idea. But I can say that I do not know what I would do without LaVon. I am terrible at managing details of our home, taking care of the checkbook, making sure the kids get to the doctors or eat right. She is the chief operating officer of Hamilton, Inc.

As an aside, we men often take our wives for granted in this area. Instead of expressing and demonstrating our appreciation, we do not say anything. As noted in the last chapter, it is critical that men take the time to express appreciation for this gift, even as they seek to partner in sharing these responsibilities.

Sexual Intimacy

One of the top five ways married men in their thirties, forties, and fifties reported feeling most loved was in the area of sexual intimacy. (Men younger and older overwhelmingly wrote that this was a "very important" part of their life but did not rank it as highly.) Here is an example of a typical comment: "When my wife initiates this, when she loves me in this way, I feel close to her. I feel her sharing herself with me." Willard Harley verifies our findings in his book *His Needs, Her Needs,* in which he indicates that sexual intimacy is one of the most powerful needs of most men, if not *the* most powerful.[4]

Interestingly, while the married men we surveyed did not generally list this at the top of their needs list, they reported that when the need is not being met, there are dire consequences. We will discuss this issue in more detail in Chapter 6, "God's Plan for Sexual Intimacy." In that chapter we will explore the role of sex, clearly intended by God to be a wonderful and emotionally bonding experience.

I would add that married men, like married women, also expressed appreciation of the times when their spouses touch them in nonsexual ways. Many husbands said how much they appreciate their wives' hugs, kisses, gentle touches, and backrubs. For both sexes, touch is an important part of expressing love.

Quality Time Doing Things Together

Finally, married men reported feeling closest to their wives when they spend quality time doing things together.

In the previous chapter we learned that wives expressed a similar need. Note, however, a key difference: While women wanted quality time to share feelings, men seemed to be thinking more of activities, things to do together. Husbands were seeking what Willard Harley calls "recreational companionship" from their mates.[5]

But many of the married men also were expressing something else. They wanted their wives to make time for them. This was particularly prevalent among men with small children, who, despite loving their children deeply, sometimes feel that the children are more important to their wives than they are and that the relationship suffers as a result. The men in this group expressed a desire for balance and for both husband and wife to carve out time for each other.

What Married Men Do Not Want

As we did with married women, we asked married men what they would change about their mates. The list was not nearly so long as the list generated by the married women. Furthermore, the second most frequently given answer was "nothing."

Those who did give responses expressed a wish for their wives to be less stressed. One man noted after his answer, "Of course, I understand, I am the one who makes her that way!" Another frequently given answer was that husbands wanted their wives to be more positive and encouraging and less critical. One man noted, "A little word of encouragement once in a while would go a long way."

What Single Men Want

One hundred fifty single men of all ages returned our survey as well. We asked them, "What do you find most appealing or attractive in a woman?" I will share with you what the men in their thirties said, as this group was fairly representative of the rest. These men said that the number-one thing they look for in a potential mate is a woman of faith! In fact, seventy-three percent of men in their thirties indicated that this was important. Here are the top six items they listed:

1. Christian faith
2. Attractive looks
3. Sense of humor
4. Intelligence
5. Similar interests
6. Strong morals

Just a word about men's interest in women's physical appearance: It is true that men are very visual creatures, and it is true that men's attention is drawn to women who are beautiful. As an illustration, LaVon and I were sitting in a restaurant some time ago and a woman walked in who caused every man in that room to turn and stare. She was dressed provocatively; and when I looked at her, I found it hard to look away. I did look away, however, because to stare would be disrespectful to my wife and to God. And although the woman may have been dressed to attract such attention, it was disrespectful to the woman as well. We men struggle with this.

But here is something else to consider, ladies: The most attractive women I know are not perfect "10s" when it comes to their physical appearance. The attractiveness of such women comes from within—from their hearts and their ways of caring—which creates a certain mystique about them. Most men have learned what the writer of Proverbs said:

"Beauty is fleeting, / but a woman who fears the LORD is to be praised" (Proverbs 31:30, NIV).

What Single Men Do Not Want

What makes a woman unattractive? According to the same group of single men in their thirties, whose responses again were fairly typical of the one hundred fifty single men surveyed, the following characteristics, in order of importance, are most unattractive in a woman:

1. Insecure/needy/low self-esteem
2. Conceited
3. Not caring for body/hygiene/appearance
4 Smoking
5. Disrespectful
6. Bad/negative attitude
7. Lying

Three Not-So-Secret Secrets About Men

Men have their secrets, and our group was willing to share some of theirs. When we asked what they thought women should know about men, here is what they said:

We need our down time.

In *Men Are From Mars, Women Are From Venus,* John Gray refers to this as "cave time." We men need to have a bit of time (some of us when we first get home from work, some of us late at night or during the weekend) when our minds can wander and we can become lost in our thoughts. For some men, the "cave" is a workbench. For others, it is a backyard. For still others, it is a motorcycle or tractor. Women, this does not mean we do not love you or want to share with you. It is simply our way of processing our thoughts, just as many of you process your thoughts by talking about them.

Tell women not to expect us to read their minds!

Ladies, when you want us to know something, please tell us! We are not mind readers. For example, when you get your hair colored 1/24th of a shade different from the previous color, do not wait for us to notice and then get irritated when we do not say anything. Just tell us you changed your hair color; we will be happy to tell you how beautiful it looks! But you are setting both of us up for a fall if you do not tell us what is on your mind.

Inside, we would like to be the knight in shining armor that you have dreamed of.

We would like for you to be proud of us. We do not want you to be overly needy; we would not know what to do with that. But we would like for you to need us, think well of us, and believe that we make a difference in your life.

The Most Controversial Scripture of the Last Thirty Years

I would like to return for a moment to the premise of this book: God made us different and created the idea of marriage. God's plan was that men and women would complement one another and help meet one another's needs for companionship. I have noted that marriage is a mutual ministry. When we marry, we are called by God to help meet the needs of our mates. Among the greatest needs mentioned by the men in my congregation, and by most men in my experience, is the need to be admired and affirmed.

I feel this in my relationship with LaVon. She is not some wild-eyed admirer; in fact, at times she is my most vocal critic. But she also believes in me. She encourages me. She has made me the man I am today. She has done this, not by constantly criticizing my shortcomings, but by carefully watching when I do something right and praising me for it. (I have noticed that she uses the same technique to train our beagle puppy!) Over the years, both she and I have come to realize that the words that make me feel most supported and appreciated by her are not "I love you," though those are very important, but "I am proud of you."

With this in mind, let's examine our Scripture passage. I want to begin by recognizing that for generations this passage has been misused and abused, leading in some cases to the oppression of women. During the past thirty years there has been an understandable backlash, in which some women have condemned this passage of Scripture and a few have even suggested excising it from the Bible.

But let's look again. It seems to me that once we get past the misconceptions and misinterpretations, this passage contains some important truths; and we ignore them at our own peril.

Let's start by acknowledging the fact that Paul's use of the word *submit,* which is found in several translations, is not as helpful as it once may have been. Perhaps if he were alive today, he would use a different word. But the underlying message is important. Eugene Peterson translates the passage in this way:

Out of respect for Christ, be courteously reverent to one another. Wives, understand and support your husbands in ways that show your support for Christ. The husband provides leadership to his wife the way Christ does to his church, not by domineering but by cherishing. So just as the church submits to Christ as he exercises such leadership, wives should likewise submit to their husbands. (Ephesians 5:21-24)[6]

Dr. Elizabeth Achtemeir, Professor of Bible at Union Theological Seminary, writes of the passage,

Certainly this does not mean that wives are to worship their husbands, to obey them unquestioningly, or to elevate them to the place of God.... Rather, wives are to act toward their husbands as the church should act toward Christ—in faithfulness, in love, in service, in honor, in devotion—because what the wife does to her husband she is in fact doing to Christ. If she is unfaithful, nagging, complacent or hostile toward him, she so treats her Lord."[7]

In our home, here is what the passage from Ephesians looks like in action: We have a mutual submission to each other. I love LaVon sacrificially. She honors and treats me with respect—not as one who is better or smarter or holier than she is, but as one who is committed to laying down his life for her. She knows that I would do anything for her and that I strive to love her as Christ loves the church.

Men, in order to be honored and deserving of a wife who is willing to be subject to you (remembering that you also are subject to her), you must be worthy of her respect; and you must love her as Christ loved the church. A marriage based on this model requires both sides of the equation, a husband who loves as Christ does and seeks to meet the needs of his wife and a wife who honors as the church does and seeks to meet the needs of her husband.

I realize that some married women find it hard to honor and respect their husbands. If you are in this group, I have a word of advice: Try looking for one thing, just one, for which you can praise your husband. Try building him up and encouraging him with your words. You have great power over him, yet you must understand that your power does not come through criticism; it comes through praise.

Relationships are complicated. Men and women are different, and they are complex. These are some of the reasons marriage is not easy. But as we learn to be "courteously reverent" to one another and build up one another, we begin to develop habits that allow our love to last a lifetime.

---

[1] From *The Five Love Languages,* by Gary Chapman (Northfield Publishers, 1992); page 40.

[2] From *His Needs, Her Needs,* by Willard Harley (Fleming H. Revell Co., 1988); page 131.

[3] From *The Five Love Languages,* by Gary Chapman; page 87.

[4] From *His Needs, Her Needs,* by Willard Harley; page 42.

[5] From *His Needs, Her Needs,* by Willard Harley; page 75.

[6] From *The Message,* by Eugene H. Peterson (NavPress, 2002).

[7] From *The Committed Marriage,* by Elizabeth Achtemeier (Westminster Press, 1976); page 85.

Personal Reflection

Individuals
- Look over the list of what makes men feel loved. Men: Which of these are you most in need of? Women: Which of these do you need to work on?
- Women only: Read 1 Corinthians 13:1-8a. Insert your name in the place of "love" and "it" in verses 4-7 to see how you measure up to God's desires.
- Women only: List all the things about the man you love that are unique, special, or praiseworthy. What about his character is good? What does he do that makes a difference? Write him a note of encouragement and thanks. Leave it for him to read when he has some alone time.
- Wives only: Read Ephesians 5:21-24, 33. How can you communicate respect and honor to your husband?

Couples
- Sit down together and discuss your responses to the first bulleted point above. Women: Ask, "What can I do for you to bless and encourage you? When do you feel closest to me? Are there things I do that push you away?"
- Women: Plan to do something as a couple this week that *he* enjoys doing.

CHAPTER 4

After the Honeymoon Is Over

As God's chosen ones, holy and beloved, clothe yourselves with compassion, kindness, humility, meekness, and patience. Bear with one another and, if anyone has a complaint against another, forgive each other; just as the Lord has forgiven you, so you also must forgive. Above all, clothe yourselves with love, which binds everything together in perfect harmony.

(Colossians 3:12-14)

Eventually every honeymoon comes to an end, and that is when marriage truly begins. Marriage is meant to last a lifetime, but often there are ups and downs on the rocky road of love. As we continue our exploration of love, marriage, and sex, we will discuss what happens to a marriage when confronted by the everyday pressures of life and the joyful but stressful pressures of starting a family. We will present strategies for rekindling the flames of love in a relationship. And we will explore some biblical principles that can help make love last and help strengthen a marriage.

Falling Out of Love

When LaVon and I first fell in love, it was wonderful—euphoric. We were high school sweethearts. We laughed together, cried together, talked and played together. We felt God calling us to marriage; and we wed right out of high school, over twenty years ago. We married in the afternoon at the local church. The first sign that things would not necessarily go as planned was that, as we drove away to begin our honeymoon, LaVon burst into tears. I thought to myself, "What have I just done?"

The early years of our marriage were characterized by wonderful and fun times, as well as by frustrating and disappointing times. Both of us had preconceived ideas of what marriage would be like and what each other would be like. She was neat; I was, well, let's just say not as neat. I thought women were as interested in physical intimacy as men. She thought men might be a bit more romantic. Most difficult of all, our marriage, which both of us had longed for and were so enthusiastic about, settled into the mundane routines of everyday life—doing laundry, fixing dinner, trying to make ends meet with very little income. We lived in a 700-square-foot apartment with no place to get away from each other. She worked full time; I worked half time and went to college. We had a solid marriage, but it certainly was not as exciting as we had expected!

Four years went by, and during that time our love grew. We worked through challenges, began to discover how to love each other, and started discerning each other's love language. We grew closer than ever during LaVon's pregnancy with our first child, Danielle. Then Danielle was born, and everything changed. No one had quite prepared us for this. Having a child was exhilarating, wonderful, and exciting; but it was also stressful, exhausting, and emotionally draining. During that time we faced what, according to psychologist John Gottman, approximately two-thirds of all couples face in the aftermath of having children: We experienced a significant change in our feelings for each other.[1]

Here is how I would put it: LaVon and I fell out of love. We still were committed to each other. We had married each other for better or for worse—and this was not so bad. I did not dislike her; but I felt no romantic feelings for her, no deep love for or closeness to her. We shared a home, a bed, and a child, bound together by a promise made nearly five years earlier.

At that point, as at several other junctures, our marriage could have gone one of two ways. It was entirely possible that we might have continued to drift apart, would never have recovered our love, and either would have agreed simply to cohabit—to live together for the sake of our commitments to God and our child, an approach that is quite common in marriages today—or we might have decided we were no longer in love and sought to part on amicable terms, agreeing always to be friends and seeking to find terms upon which we could share the upbringing of our daughter. A third alternative was to learn to rekindle the flame in our relationship and have a marriage that was stronger than ever.

We took the third path, though we really did not understand it at the time. We learned to fall back in love. I would like to share with you some of what we, and others, have learned about what it takes to revive a faltering marriage. I also will offer you a few key principles of successful marriages, gleaned from the work of one prominent psychologist in this field. Finally, I will examine the relationship between the Scripture passage before us and the marriage relationship.

Gottman's Principles for Making Marriages Work

Let's take a moment to consider the work of John Gottman, the psychologist whose work I referred to previously. Gottman, Professor Emeritus of Psychology at the University of Washington and author of several books on marriage, has spent years studying couples and trying to determine what works and what does not work in marriage.

Some of Gottman's ideas are a bit unorthodox. One claim that has brought him notoriety is that he can predict, within five minutes of observing a couple in his laboratory, whether the couple will divorce in the future—and he says that so far he has done this with ninety-one percent accuracy.

Other aspects of Gottman's work may be more useful to us. His book *The Seven Principles for Making Marriage Work* was a *New York Times* best seller. I believe that this book (co-authored with Nan Silver) and his volume *Why Marriages Succeed or Fail* contain a great deal of helpful information for couples.

In his books, Gottman submits that much of the traditional wisdom about how to improve marriages is just plain wrong. He disagrees with experts who focus on conflict-resolution techniques (learning to "fight" constructively) and instead suggests another approach, based on positive rather than negative interactions.

Gottman asserts that in a successful marriage there must be more positive than negative feelings, words, and experiences flowing between partners; and he indicates that the magic ratio is five to one. That is, for every conflict there should be five positive affirmations of friendship and love. This leads us to a major premise of Gottman's work: The key to reviving or "divorce-proofing" a marriage is not in how you resolve conflict or disagreements but in "how you are with each other when you're not fighting."[2]

Gottman's concept is that if you can cultivate a friendship with your mate and in that friendship apply the following principles, then your marriage can thrive. I will summarize four of his seven principles for you to consider.

1. Know your mate.

One key to any friendship is learning about the other person. Gottman asserts that this is even truer of marriage. He suggests that couples must be intentional about getting to know each other's likes and dislikes, interests, thoughts, and friends.

Gottman encourages couples to work on developing "love maps" of their mates—detailed information about how they think, what they enjoy, and what is going on in their lives. He believes that out of this knowledge a sensitivity to the mate's needs will develop, as well as an ability to maintain friendship and love through the storms of life.

2. Nurture your fondness and admiration for your mate.

Gottman says it is possible to nurture fondness even if your marriage is on the rocks. When conducting marriage counseling sessions, I often encourage couples to write a letter to each other in which they describe the things about their mate that they admire, appreciate, love, and are grateful for. This focus on the positive in one's spouse can help nurture admiration, respect, or fondness.

I recall one couple who described the years following the birth of their first child and how their marriage nearly fell apart. Today they have a healthy marriage, and their love is stronger than ever. "What happened?" I asked them. They said there were two things. First, they started going to church. Second, they attended a marriage seminar where they were asked to write a letter to each other describing their love for each other, much as I do in my counseling sessions. As the couple wrote those letters and read them to each other, they rediscovered their mutual fondness and admiration.

3. Turn toward your mate and not away.

Gottman suggests that marriages that succeed do so because the spouses actually pay attention to each other, spend time acknowledging the other's comments, and connect with each other verbally. This does not necessarily mean lengthy, detailed conversations; it may be as simple as sharing a few words here and there.

Gottman observes that couples who spend time not just talking to each other but also doing simple things together have a much higher likelihood of succeeding in marriage than those who do not. He notes that success in marriage is not predicated upon the occasional super-romantic date as much as it is upon smaller, everyday things, such as going to the grocery store together, horsing around with each other, and calling from work to see how the other is doing.

4. Let your mate influence you.

This principle is directed especially toward men. Gottman notes that when a man resists his wife's influence, statistically "there is an eighty-one percent chance that his marriage will self-destruct." Gottman's study was quoted in a 1998 *Kansas City Star* article entitled "Study advises men to tell wives, 'Let's do what you say.'" I laughed when I read that story. It began, "Husbands, forget all that pyscho-babble about active listening and validation. If you want your marriage to last for a long time, the newest advice from psychologists is quite simple: Just do what your wife says."

Of course, that is an oversimplification of Gottman's point. Capitulating to your wife's desires and plans all the time is not the key to a successful marriage; the key is to allow your spouse's views and desires to influence you. As you do that, you create a partnership that enriches both persons.

If you have that kind of partnership, others will sometimes deride it, making statements such as, "I know who wears the pants in that family." Such talk is ridiculous. It means that to be a real man is to be an ignoramus, one who makes all the decisions in a vacuum, without the benefit of the person God gave him as a partner. I consider the acceptance of influence and shared decision-making not only to be essential to a healthy marriage, but to be indicative of maturity, wisdom, and genuine Christian character. It is part of God's big idea in marriage, that mates are called to be each other's helper.

My ministry in the church is what it is today because of LaVon's influence on my thoughts, plans, and even sermons. So many times she sees things I have not noticed, offers perspectives I have overlooked, has insights that I have missed. Because I solicit and honor her ideas, LaVon is invested in my work, as I am in hers; and that makes us partners. Our partnership allows my job to be something that draws us closer together rather than something that pushes us apart.

Building Christian Marriages That Last

All my friends have shortcomings, things that irritate me or things I would change. They could say the same about me. Do not expect your mate to be any different. There comes a time in a relationship when you choose to overlook your spouse's flaws and focus on the qualities that are admirable. You learn to be patient. You choose to be thankful for who your spouse is rather than focusing on who he or she is not. You act toward your mate with love, compassion, and kindness even when you do not feel that way inside; and somehow the doing of these things makes for a great friendship. It also makes for a great marriage, which takes us back to our Scripture passage.

In our Scripture passage for this chapter, the apostle Paul writes to the Christians at the town of Colossae, in what is now Turkey. Paul describes how Christians ought to treat one another. (He is not writing to husbands and wives in particular.) Paul says that if you are in Christ, this is what your life should look like: You should clothe yourselves with compassion, kindness, humility, gentleness, and patience. Bear with one another and forgive whatever grievances you may have against another. And over all these virtues, put on love, which binds them all together in perfect unity.

This is a powerful picture of what our Christian relationships should look like and how we should appear to those around us. I would add that if it is true for those around us, how much more should it be true for the one person whom God has specifically entrusted to our care? Remember that, in the Bible, marriage is a sacred calling in which God entrusts one person's soul, body, and needs to another's care. We are called to be a gift from God to our mates, and we are called to minister to them.

It may be relatively easy for me to practice these virtues toward members of my church, since I only see them once in a while. It is far more challenging to practice them at home, toward the person I live with all the time. In spite of that difficulty, or perhaps because of it, if we hear and truly practice this calling from God, our marriages will begin to soar.

Paul's words offer us a recipe for a successful friendship, a deep partnership, and a blessed marriage. But we can only follow his advice if we invite God to help. On my own I cannot be particularly patient or compassionate or forgiving; but when I am connected to Christ, when the Holy Spirit is working in me, when I am spending time in prayer, these virtues become a possibility for me.

For example, I once visited a church member whose marriage had been unraveling. He told me that things had changed dramatically in the past six months, and I noted that he was more hopeful and encouraged than I had seen him in a long time. I asked, "What made the difference?" He replied, "I took the focus off of me and what I could do to change her and began looking at how I could minister to her, and it changed everything."

Here is what happened in our marriage fifteen years ago: One night I was up late doing schoolwork, and LaVon was in bed asleep; and I was thinking of how empty I felt.

There were no more feelings of love in my heart for her. Then a thought came into my mind, the kind of strong impression that I have come to trust as God's Spirit speaking to me. This impression, this voice, said, "Get up, and go buy her flowers." It was after midnight! I did not feel like going out and buying her flowers! But the voice would not go away. I tried to work; but I kept hearing this voice saying, "Get up, and go buy her flowers." Finally I put down my work, got dressed, and drove to an all-night supermarket. I bought her a dozen roses and a card. I came home and had another strong impression that I was supposed to bless her. So I wrote several lines in the card about what I admired in her. Before I went to bed that night, I prayed for LaVon; and that night, for the first night in a long time, I began to feel love for her again.

My flowers prompted a response from her, which prompted another response from me. Each day I began looking for ways to bless her. I began praying for her— praying over and over that God would use me to bless this woman, to encourage her, to help her feel loved. While I was doing this, unbeknownst to me, she was doing the same thing. Over the course of the next few months, we fell in love again.

Here is what I learned from this experience: Our actions are not meant to follow our feelings, except perhaps at the beginning of a relationship. Rather, our feelings follow our actions. It is in doing love that we begin to feel love. Said another way, mature love is *doing* love even when you do not *feel* it. When you persistently do loving things toward another person, an amazing thing happens: The doing produces the feelings.

Love Gets You Through the Tough Times

You will not always feel love for your spouse. Some parts of marriage require something much deeper than feelings. They require a commitment to love, a commitment to following Christ in serving this other human being.

I have seen this principle at work in the lives of many church members whom I have had the privilege of serving during difficult times. I have watched these people, and I have seen the most profound pictures of what marriage is meant to be. I saw God's grace at work in the way a husband ministered to his wife as she died of cancer and in the way a wife loved and cared for her husband as he was dying of ALS. It was not easy. It was sometimes very, very hard. Yet God used these two people to bless their mates and, in profound ways, used their mates to bless and transform them.

One of the most moving examples I can recall involved a prominent local pastor who served his congregation for over twenty years. His wife was his partner and friend. She had been a beautiful woman, charming, smart, and always dressed impeccably. In her later years she contracted Alzheimer's disease. By the time I met her, she was just a shadow of her former self.

What amazed me was that, despite her Alzheimer's, everywhere that her husband went, he made sure she was still by his side. Every morning he awakened his wife and got her ready for the day. He put on her makeup, dressed her in the most beautiful of clothes, prepared her hair, and off they went as partners—for years until her passing. This kind of love was not easy. It was not filled with deposits to his love bank. This kind of behavior is not always possible, but this man's care for his wife demonstrated something profoundly Christian. It presented a picture of what marriage is meant to be: two people faithfully loving and serving each other until God calls one or the other home.

If you have unclear expectations of marriage and how it is to be lived, it is important that you read these words: Marital love begins and ends with friendship and a commitment to do love even when you do not feel it. You may be married and your love has grown cold. Perhaps you have children and you have "lost that loving feeling." This is a normal part of any marriage relationship. Your situation is not hopeless. It is possible to fall in love again.

It is often said that John Wesley, the founder of Methodism, used to tell his ministers to "preach faith until you have it." I encourage you to *practice love until you feel it.* There is hope for every marriage. What you may feel now will pass, but only if you are committed to that profound calling you accepted in your marriage vows: "for better, for worse, for richer, for poorer, in sickness and in health, to love and to cherish, until we are parted by death."[3]

As Paul says in Colossians, "Clothe yourselves with love." It is what you need to be wearing after the honeymoon is over to make love last a lifetime.

---

[1] See *The Seven Principles for Making Marriage Work,* by John Gottman (Three Rivers Press, 2000); page 49.
[2] From *The Seven Principles for Making Marriage Work,* by John Gottman; page 46.
[3] From *The United Methodist Hymnal* (Copyright © 1989 The United Methodist Publishing House); 867.

Personal Reflection

Individuals
- Meditate on Colossians 3:12-14. How would your relationship be different if you were able to live this out more fully?
- A man whose marriage had been unraveling said that things changed dramatically when he took the focus off himself and what he could do to change his wife and he began looking at how he could minister to her. Prayerfully consider how you can minister to the man or woman you love, and begin doing some of these things this week.
- Read Matthew 7:1-5. What are the implications for a love relationship found in this passage? Is there a speck in anyone's eye that you have been trying to remove? What are the logs in your own eye?
- Read the First Letter of John (near the end of the New Testament). What in this letter speaks to you? What do you learn about love from this letter?

Couples
- Author John Gottman encourages couples to work on developing "love maps" of each other—detailed information about how each person thinks, what each person enjoys, and what is going on in each person's life. Go somewhere you enjoy being together, and begin compiling your own "love maps." Have fun with this!
- Discuss and list ways you can cultivate your friendship. Choose one to begin working on this week.

CHAPTER 5

The Habits of Unhealthy Marriages

So then, putting away falsehood, let all of us speak the truth to our neighbors, for we are members of one another. Be angry but do not sin; do not let the sun go down on your anger, and do not make room for the devil.... Let no evil talk come out of your mouths, but only what is useful for building up, as there is need, so that your words may give grace to those who hear. And do not grieve the Holy Spirit of God, with which you were marked with a seal for the day of redemption. Put away from you all bitterness and wrath and anger and wrangling and slander, together with all malice, and be kind to one another, tenderhearted, forgiving one another, as God in Christ has forgiven you.

(Ephesians 4:25-32)

All of us have bad habits, things we do that are not healthy or that annoy our partners. That is because we are human. Some people smoke, eat too much, drive too fast, or occasionally use bad language; but these habits are not necessarily fatal to a marriage. Then there is the bad stuff—I mean the really bad stuff—that is sometimes so awful we try to ignore it. We hope it will go away. But it does not. We need to deal with it.

I am referring to what I call the five habits of unhealthy marriages. These are five issues that easily can destroy a relationship. They constitute the issues that, in my experience counseling couples over the past fifteen years, lead many married couples to divorce. My goal is to encourage you to recognize these problems when they occur in your relationship and seek help in coping with them.

We will end by looking at one essential good habit of a successful and lasting marriage. But first we begin with the bad stuff.

1. Disrespect, Contempt, Criticism, and Abuse

We have seen the need for spouses to admire each other. The opposite of admiring others is showing them contempt and disrespect, despising them, criticizing or tearing them down constantly. Neither men nor women can thrive in a marriage in which they are treated in this way.

People of both sexes are guilty of this kind of behavior. Women report that they hate it when their husbands treat them patronizingly or as though they were not equal partners in the marriage. Likewise, I have watched many a wife look down on her husband, see only his shortcomings, freely speak ill of him, or constantly criticize him.

Please avoid this kind of behavior at all costs. It does not reflect the love of Christ. I firmly believe that if you cannot find something to respect in your mate, you will never find true love. I have met only a handful of people in whom I could find nothing to admire or praise.

Sometimes spouses live into what we say about them. A husband who is constantly told that he is a failure will eventually live like one. Conversely, husbands and wives whose mates speak highly of them, who experience five times more encouragement than criticism (as described in Chapter 4), generally will seek to live up to that praise.

Read the words of the apostle Paul in Romans 12:10: "Love one another with mutual affection; outdo one another in showing honor." Imagine a marriage in which both parties outdo each other in showing honor. What might that look like? How might you lead the way?

A related issue that destroys marriages must be mentioned at this point. The issue is verbal and physical abuse. Some of you, both men and women, struggle with anger control and poor self-esteem, resulting in frequent outbursts in which you threaten your mate, demean your mate, or in some cases physically harm your mate or your children. Most of you know that this is wrong. When you are done with your outburst, you feel great sorrow and remorse. But the next time something sets you off, you cannot resist the impulse to repeat the abusive behavior.

I am going to tell you something that you probably know already; nevertheless, it must be said. This behavior is destroying the person you are married to and likely will have a devastating impact upon your children.

You have been entrusted with preserving the health and well-being of your mate. When you are abusive, you are doing exactly the opposite; you are destroying your mate. This is not a marriage; it is a nightmare, even when there are positive interludes. I have counseled with persons, primarily women, whose spouses called them vile names, sought to control every part of their lives, and treated them with such hatred and contempt that I felt anger welling up inside toward the perpetrator of such abuse. Such stories help me understand the biblical concept of the wrath of God.

Our passage of Scripture is clear in speaking both to ordinary couples and to those with anger control issues and a history of abuse:

> Let no evil talk come out of your mouths, but only what is useful for building up, as there is need, so that your words may give grace to those who hear. And do not grieve the Holy Spirit of God, with which you were marked with a seal for the day of redemption. Put away from you all bitterness and wrath and anger and wrangling and slander, together with all malice, and be kind to one another.
>
> (Ephesians 4:29-32)

If you struggle with these kinds of issues—you cannot seem to control yourself or keep yourself from physically or verbally abusing your mate—then you must get help. Participating in counseling with a specialist in this area can help you find techniques to control your abusive tendencies and to bring real change, techniques you would be unlikely to find and develop on your own. If you want to be the man or woman God wishes you to be, if you want to have a love that will last a lifetime, then get help.

2. Dishonesty and Lying

A second deadly habit is dishonesty and lying. Marriage is a relationship based upon trust. When persons lie to their spouses, it undermines the very foundation of the relationship. In marriage we entrust our secrets, our thoughts, our heart, to another. Lying to a spouse not only betrays that trust; it ultimately leads to contempt and then to emotional separation.

In Proverbs 6:16-19, we read that "there are six things that the LORD hates, / seven that are an abomination to him." Two of these are a "lying tongue" and a witness who tells lies. Proverbs 10:18 notes that "lying lips conceal hatred." Proverbs 12:22 states, "Lying lips are an abomination to the LORD." The prophets of ancient Israel repeatedly denounce the people for their lies and deceitfulness, as in Isaiah 59:13, where the people are condemned for "conceiving lying words and uttering them from the heart." Paul writes in Colossians 3:9-10, "Do not lie to one another, seeing that you have stripped off the old self with its practices and have clothed yourselves with the new self, which is being renewed in knowledge according to the image of its creator."

Again and again, the Bible confirms what we know from instinct and experience: A marriage cannot withstand the onslaught of dishonesty and deceit. No relationship can.

3. Poor Handling of Money

There are few things that have as much power to destroy a healthy relationship as money. This is particularly true when we are faced with debt, often a result of trying to live beyond our means. I have seen marriages that otherwise would have been successful come apart when the couple failed to plan their finances as a team or when they struggled to make ends meet.

Most couples have occasional conflicts about money, often stemming from differences over spending and saving habits. My wife, LaVon, sometimes drives me crazy with her fiscal conservatism; but over the years I have come to appreciate this quality in her. Her conservative instincts are one reason we have what we have today. At the same time, my willingness to take certain risks and my eye for a good investment, though at times stressful for her, have helped us build wealth over time. In other words, our very differences in this area are a gift from God and, even though sometimes they lead to conflict, are a way of providing balance in our marriage.

I would lift up to you two biblical principles with regard to finances. The first principle is found in Ecclesiastes 5:10: "The lover of money will not be satisfied with money; nor the lover of wealth, with gain. This also is vanity." The principle is stated somewhat differently by Paul in 1 Timothy 6:9-10:

Those who want to be rich fall into temptation and are trapped by many senseless and harmful desires that plunge people into ruin and destruction. For the love of money is a root of all kinds of evil, and in their eagerness to be rich some have wandered away from the faith and pierced themselves with many pains.

I would restate the principle in this way: Be careful about what you consider really important in your life. Money and possessions are fine; they are not evil in themselves. The importance you ascribe to them, the value you place upon them, and the purposes for which you use them determine whether they are good or evil.

The second biblical principle is tithing. Tithing is the practice of making offerings to God from the first of what we have, not the last. The Bible teaches that the first tenth of what we earn is claimed by God. It is not meant to be ours. This biblical principle is intended to provide resources for God's work, while also serving to bless us and to help us keep our priorities in line.

LaVon and I lived at the national poverty level the first year we were married. I recall eating supper out just once during the first six months of our marriage. We drove old cars. We bought generic label groceries. But the first check we wrote each month was our tithe—ten percent of our income—given to the church for God's work. In this way we put God first in our lives, prioritized our finances, and received great joy. Every year our savings seemed to grow, so that by the time we graduated from seminary, we actually had ten thousand dollars in the bank!

Live within your means, not on credit. Do not seek to use money, expenditures, or possessions as a means of building your self-esteem, impressing others, or trying to fill the emptiness in your life. That emptiness can only be filled by God. Putting God first in your life, as symbolized by your tithes and offerings, will have a tremendous impact upon your marriage.

4. Alcohol and Drugs

Perhaps it is obvious, but few things can destroy a marriage more surely than alcohol abuse and drug use. This behavior usually does not result in the sudden death of a marriage; more often, the death is slow and painful. Many times those abusing alcohol or drugs do not even believe they have a problem.

73

If your mate says that you have a problem, you must listen. You may not believe you are an alcoholic or a drug addict; but if the person closest to you is being affected, then your substance use is interfering with your relationship.

With only a small amount of alcohol or drugs in your system, your personality can change. From your perspective, the changes may seem positive. You become more relaxed, the edge is taken off, and the stress begins to dissipate. But those around you may see the changes quite differently. Sometimes your actions may seem annoying or disappointing, sometimes embarrassing, sometimes frightening.

I once knew a twelve-year-old boy who came home from school each day to find his stepfather and friends drinking. They were having a great time getting intoxicated. The boy was terrified, however. His stepfather, whom he really loved, came home one evening in an angry, drunken rage and took a sledgehammer to the walls of the house. Meanwhile the boy, his sister, and his mother sat at the dinner table trying to eat supper, pretending there was nothing wrong. This marriage did not survive. And though this is an extreme example, it did not start off so seriously. This boy's stepfather was a great guy, but he became someone different when he drank.

I have seen too many marriages destroyed because spouses were unwilling to listen and to understand the impact that alcohol or drug use was having on those who loved them the most.

The Bible does not forbid drinking alcohol; in fact, the drinking of wine is presented as a part of life throughout the Scripture. At the same time, however, Proverbs 20:1 notes, "Wine is a mocker, strong drink a brawler, / and whoever is led astray by it is not wise."

Many in our culture seem dependent on alcohol in order to have a "good time." Fifty-three percent of men and women in the United States report that one or more of their close relatives has a drinking problem.[1] If you think you might have a problem with alcohol or someone says that you might have a problem even if you do not think so, you might want to check out the information at www.niaaa.nih.gov/publications/booklet.htm, where you will find a helpful online pamphlet entitled "Alcoholism: Getting the Facts." It is difficult to make love last a lifetime when alcohol or drug abuse is a part of the equation.

5. Infidelity

Of all the vices we have mentioned, the one that most surely will destroy a marriage is infidelity. Having a physically or emotionally intimate relationship outside of marriage is utterly destructive to marriage. For this reason every portion of the Bible—the Law, the Prophets, the Writings, the Gospels, and the Epistles—condemns extramarital affairs.

In marriage, two people are bound together—in every way. The physical relationship is intended to represent and strengthen this bonding. When a man or woman becomes intimate with someone outside the marriage, the original bond is torn and the person becomes double-bonded. This has devastating consequences on that person's mate.

Several couples whom I interviewed in preparation for this book had experienced the pain of infidelity. In addition, I have counseled more than a dozen church members who have committed adultery; and I know there are hundreds of others. If you can imagine pouring poison or acid on the soul of your mate, you begin to understand the impact of infidelity. But your mate is not the only one damaged; so are your children. One woman I know is still in therapy, ten years later, as a result of the betrayal she experienced when her father had an extramarital affair.

In addition, infidelity is a cancer on your own soul. The act of committing adultery, or taking steps in that direction emotionally, will eat away at you. You will discover that those few moments of pleasure can haunt you for the rest of your life.

I will discuss infidelity in more detail later in this book. For now I simply want to acknowledge that it is among the most destructive things that can happen to a marriage. For this reason, despite Jesus' very high standards regarding the marriage commitment, he allows for divorce in cases of infidelity (Matthew 5:31-32).

Two Key Biblical Principles

Before moving to the one habit that every effective marriage must cultivate, allow me to offer two key biblical principles that Jesus offers to us. Together they form an overarching ethic or guide to the treatment of our mates or anyone else we meet. The first principle is what we know as Jesus' "Golden Rule." Burn it in your heart: "Do unto others as you would have them do unto you." The second is Jesus' "law of love": "Love your neighbor as you love yourself." Applying these two New Testament principles would eliminate nearly all the habits of unhealthy marriages.

Now, let's move from these negative habits to one positive habit that no marriage can survive without: the habit of practicing forgiveness.

Forgiveness: Living a Marriage Filled With Grace

You may have experienced the pain of having a mate practice one of the five habits of unhealthy marriages. You may have stepped across the line yourself. Even if you have not, there will be times, weekly if not daily, when you will say or do something that is hurtful to your mate or your mate will say or do something that is hurtful to you. I guarantee it.

That is the reason why no marriage can survive without the frequent use of six magic words. The three most important words must be spoken first: "I am sorry." And three other words must follow, sometime after the first: "I forgive you."

Forgiveness is in many ways the central theme of the Christian faith. It is what Christianity offers the world. It was Jesus' response to the failure of human beings to live as God intends. As part of our Christian faith, we acknowledge the many ways we sin against one another—in thought, in word, in what we have done, in what we have left undone—and the many ways we have sinned against God.

You and I, separately and together, have offended, wounded, spurned, and rejected God. What will God do to us? Will we get what we deserve? Or will we receive "a grace that is greater than all our sin"?[2]

God chose to demonstrate the magnitude of our sin and the great cost of mercy by allowing Jesus to be mocked, beaten, and crucified. This choice makes the reality of our brokenness absolutely clear and demonstrates the price that was paid for our forgiveness. The Scriptures speak of it in this way: "He himself bore our sins in his body on the cross" and "by his wounds you have been healed" (1 Peter 2:24).

This same Jesus, who died on the cross for us, taught us to pray for forgiveness by saying, "Forgive us our trespasses, as we forgive those who trespass against us." This same Jesus, when asked how many times we should forgive someone who sins against us, said, "Not seven times, but, I tell you, seventy times seven!"

Yet, in spite of this overwhelming and ever-present grace, we find it hard to forgive those who sin against us, especially when they have sinned again and again and again. Sometimes their sins are so painful to us that we cannot find it in our hearts to forgive. Why should we?

Allow me to answer the question with a story by Philip Yancey from his excellent book *What's So Amazing About Grace?* Yancey writes about Larry Trapp, who in 1992 was the Grand Dragon of the Ku Klux Klan in Lincoln, Nebraska. Trapp made headlines when he turned his back on the hate-filled life he had lived, destroyed his KKK propaganda, and took down his Nazi flags. What brought about such a radical change in Trapp's life? It was the grace and love of a Jewish cantor and his family.

Trapp had sent to the cantor's home his hate-filled literature that denied the Holocaust and mocked the Jewish people. Trapp had threatened the cantor's family and had planned to bomb their synagogue. But the family always responded to Trapp by offering blessings and love for every act of hatred.

Toward the end of his life, Trapp was going blind and was confined to a wheelchair. The cantor and his family invited Trapp to their home to care for him. Trapp said, "They showed me such love that I couldn't help but love them back." Consequently the final months of his life were spent asking for forgiveness from those he had wronged.

Larry Trapp was transformed by the power of forgiveness and grace.

When you choose to harbor bitterness and resentment, you destroy your own soul; and you miss an opportunity to transform another person by the power of grace.

Should everyone be forgiven the moment they ask for it? Perhaps not. There may be value in asking for genuine penitence before grace is offered. Such penitence need not involve punishment, and it certainly should not imply that grace can be earned. But there may be acts on the part of the sinners—restitution, for example—that will help them understand the magnitude of what they have done and help the victims be healed.

Sometimes, however, grace is simply offered, even before forgiveness is asked for, in order to transform the one in need of it. In the extending of grace, the person sinned against is often released from bitterness and pain and thus also transformed.

Which takes us back to our Scripture passage from Ephesians 4:

Let no evil talk come out of your mouths, but only what is useful for building up, as there is need, so that your words may give grace to those who hear. And do not grieve the Holy Spirit of God, with which you were marked with a seal for the day of redemption. Put away from you all bitterness and wrath and anger and wrangling and slander, together with all malice, and be kind to one another, tenderhearted, forgiving one another, as God in Christ has forgiven you.

(Ephesians 4:29-32)

Forgiveness is an essential habit of any highly effective marriage.

Freeing yourself from the destructive habits of defective marriages and freely extending the six important words— "I am sorry" and "I forgive you"—are critically important to cultivating a love that lasts a lifetime.

---

[1] See http://www.cdphp.com/home/newsroom/early_Detection.asp
[2] From "Grace Greater Than Our Sin," in *The United Methodist Hymnal* (Copyright © 1989 The United Methodist Publishing House); 365.

Personal Reflection

Individuals

- Read Romans 12:9-10. Imagine a relationship in which both parties outdo each other in showing honor. What might that look like? How might you lead the way?
- Read Ephesians 4:26-27, 29-32. Use these verses as an outline for prayer. If you have difficulty controlling your anger or are physically or verbally abusive, counseling is an important step in overcoming this habit.
- Read Proverbs 6:16-19, 12:22, and Colossians 3:9-10. How does lying undermine the security of a relationship as well as your integrity and your relationship with Christ? In what ways do you or have you struggled with dishonesty?
- Read Proverbs 20:1 and Ephesians 5:18. Are there times when alcohol or drugs are an issue for you? Do loved ones ever express concern in this area?
- The apostle Paul warns, "Don't allow love to turn into lust, setting off a downhill slide into sexual promiscuity" (Ephesians 5:3, *The Message,* NT). What are some of the ways we allow love to turn into lust? How can you guard against this?
- Read Ephesians 4:29-32 and Matthew 18:15-35. What are the implications of these passages for your life?

Couples

- All couples disagree about money from time to time. Problems arise when we regularly overspend or misuse money to meet our own needs. Read Malachi 3:8-10, Luke 12:13-34, and 1 Timothy 6:9-10. Discuss ways you can put God first in your money management practices.

- Discuss any of the other habits that are causing problems in your relationship. Consider steps each of you can take to address these concerns.
- Prayerfully consider the ways you need to seek and offer forgiveness to each other, asking the Holy Spirit to enable you to extend and receive forgiveness. Agree to let go of past hurts and allow Christ's love and mercy to bring healing and reconciliation where needed.

CHAPTER 6

God's Plan for Sexual Intimacy

Therefore a man leaves his father and his mother and clings to his wife, and they become one flesh. And the man and his wife were both naked, and were not ashamed.

(Genesis 2:24-25)

For this is the will of God, your sanctification: that you abstain from fornication; that each one of you know how to control your own body in holiness and honor, not with lustful passion, like the Gentiles who do not know God; that no one wrong or exploit a brother or sister in this matter, because the Lord is an avenger in all these things, just as we have already told you beforehand and solemnly warned you. For God did not call us to impurity but in holiness. Therefore whoever rejects this rejects not human authority but God, who also gives his Holy Spirit to you.

(1 Thessalonians 4:3-8)

Sexual intimacy is a hot commodity today. Everybody wants it. It is promoted in songs, in movies, and on television. Many advertisements are sexual in nature. Our cul-

ture is so immersed in confusing views about sexuality that what I am about to share with you may seem quite Victorian or even ridiculous. Yet no matter what you may think of it, what I am about to tell you is a timeless truth. It is a truth that will give you a glimpse of what sexuality was meant to be, rather than the cheapened, watered-down imitation being presented in the media.

The plain truth is that many of us have fallen short of God's plan for our lives when it comes to sexual intimacy. We have shut God out of that portion of our lives. The good news is that, through Christ, we can begin again and have a fresh start. God wants us to experience the gift of sexual intimacy the way it was intended to be.

Let's begin with the basic premise of the Bible regarding sex: Sex is God's idea. God designed us to be male and female, intended our differences to bring pleasure, and gave us our biological and emotional drives. In Genesis 1, God looked at all creation, including human beings, and saw that "it was very good" (1:31).

The Song of Solomon gives us a beautiful, and graphic, picture of sensual love between a man and a woman. This book's presence in the Bible serves to counter a tendency among religious people to believe that sex is bad. Sexual intimacy is not bad. It is a thing of beauty. It is not meant to produce guilt; it is meant to produce joy.

Yet it is important to understand that, as is the case with all God's gifts, God has a purpose in mind for sexual intimacy. The Bible can serve as a guidebook for use of this and many other gifts. When we understand and follow God's plan for physical intimacy, the gift becomes a blessing. But when we misuse the gift, the consequences can be tragic.

When I was a child, my mother helped me plant a small garden behind our house. I was probably in second or third grade. I had a little spade that I used to dig holes for the plants. I cannot tell you why, but one day I thought to myself, *I wonder what would happen if I put the sharp point of the spade into an electrical outlet.* I was only seven years old, yet I still remember that moment. Sparks jumped out, black smoke spread across the outlet, and the lights went out in the Hamilton home. Only the rubber handle kept me from killing myself. The spade was a good gift, a tool that had a purpose. But when it was put to the wrong use, it could have killed me. This is true of sexual intimacy as well.

God's First Purpose for Sexual Intimacy: Procreation

It is important to understand God's primary purposes for creating us as sexual beings. In the first two chapters of Genesis, we find God's plans for this part of our lives. We discover in 1:28 that the man and woman were to "be fruitful and multiply." We know that sexual intercourse was first designed as the method for procreation—making babies. How amazing it is that God created us in such a way that we can be co-creators with God!

Sexual intercourse is meant to be a holy act in which we participate with God in creation. It is part of the mystery and wonder of life. But we must understand the awesome responsibility that goes with this and be ready to accept it. Too often, perhaps because of the availability of birth control, we have forgotten this powerful purpose.

Sex is the means by which life is formed. Before you begin a sexual relationship, therefore, you must determine if you are ready to participate in the act of co-creating with God. Millions of times each year, people engage in intercourse without considering this solemn fact. They do not take into account the possibilities or consequences, and pregnancies result. Children formed in the womb are sometimes aborted, all because the sanctity of this act was not respected. Sexual intercourse is designed to be something remarkable, amazing, and awe inspiring.

God's Second Purpose for Sexual Intimacy: Bonding

It is tragic but true that religious people often have failed to understand that God, in designing us male and female, intended sexual intimacy to be more than simply a means of procreation. Even Augustine, one of the great theologians of Christianity, described sex as a necessary evil that should only be pursued for the purpose of having children.[1] That is foolishness. God made this act a pleasurable one and intended that we enjoy it as a gift throughout our lives, and not simply while we can have children.

The second purpose for this gift can be found in Genesis 2:24-25, where we read, "Therefore a man ... clings to his wife, and they become one flesh." This is a euphemistic way of describing sexual intercourse. God intended that men and women, in the context of the covenant of marriage, experience emotional bonding through the act of intercourse. This physical act corresponds to our spiritual love for one another and is meant to be another form of cement that bonds husbands and wives together for a lifetime.

Note that in this passage Adam and Eve "were both naked, and were not ashamed." God, witnessing their nakedness, saw that it was good. It was not dirty. It was not lewd. It was beautiful. In sexual intercourse the physical, emotional, and spiritual are combined in an experience of holy bonding.

But if our capacity for intimacy was designed by God to be a good thing, what happened? Why do we struggle so much with this aspect of our lives? Why is our culture so flawed in terms of how we look at sexual intimacy? I believe that the answer is to be found in our human condition. God placed within us a biological drive to reproduce; in this way we are like other animals. Yet we also have a strong emotional need for bonding, closeness, and intimacy. These two powerful drives converge in the sex act, resulting in its powerful hold over us.

Perhaps we could deal with the resulting problems and conflicts if it were not for a spiritual problem that plagues us all. Theologians call it "original sin." You might call it brokenness or a propensity to do evil. This spiritual problem manifests itself as selfishness, a desire for power and control, an insatiable hunger, a tendency toward perversion—resulting in a struggle that the apostle Paul described in his letter to the Romans: "I do not do the good I want, but the evil I do not want is what I do" (7:19).

To help clarify things, I want to focus on two of many examples of how we take God's good gifts and distort, misuse, and pervert them, thus robbing us of the joy of the gifts while potentially enslaving or harming us.

Fornication

Here I would invite you to turn to 1 Thessalonians 4:1-3, where we read,

Finally, brothers and sisters, we ask and urge you in
the Lord Jesus that, as you learned from us how you
ought to live and to please God (as, in fact, you are
doing), you should do so more and more. For you
know what instructions we gave you through the
Lord Jesus. For this is the will of God, your sanctification: that you abstain from fornication.

The word *fornication* is one we do not use much anymore. It has traditionally meant premarital sex. The Greek
word is *porneo,* which bears a broader translation than simply sexual intercourse; hence the New International Version
translates the word as "sexual immorality." If we use this
translation, it means that Paul may have been referring to
any improper sexual activity between a man and a woman,
including activities leading up to sexual intercourse.

When I was a church youth director, my teens would
ask, "How far is too far?" They wanted to know how many
"bases" they could "round" before they had gone "too far."
In answering, I was no more specific than Paul was—
except to say that fornication is not limited to sexual intercourse. It likely includes any form of genital contact.

Before addressing whether this standard is realistic,
I would like to offer you seven reasons why sex outside of
marriage is not consistent with God's plan.

1. In extra-marital sex we are not showing adequate
respect for sexual intimacy, especially considering its association with the "co-creation" of children. We are not prepared to have children, yet we want to pursue the one act
associated with their creation.

2. In extra-marital sex we are not seeking to participate in the act for the second purpose God intended: bonding and becoming one flesh. We have yet to make that commitment, through the bonds of marriage; and yet we are joining ourselves at the deepest level to another human being.

3. Our virginity is something we can give away only one time. Premarital sex robs the person we will marry of the blessing of being the first we give ourselves to in this way.

4. There is the possibility of emotional harm and pain. When the relationship ends, in effect we divorce the person with whom we have bonded.

5. Sexually transmitted diseases are being spread, even by people we trust. I once had a young woman tell me after having unprotected sex with her boyfriend that she was sure it was all right because she knew him really well. Be aware; according to the American Social Health Association, there are fifteen million new cases of sexually transmitted diseases each year. One in four sexually active teens will contract an STD,[2] which will cost some youth their lives.

6. Growing in a sexual relationship is something learned over years, with one person, in the context of a covenant relationship. It is not learned from repeated attempts to get it right with a variety of people. Such experimentation is a poor way to determine whether to commit to marry another person.

7. Relationships involving premarital sex often become primarily about the sex, thus forging bonds before promises have been made.

Is it appropriate and beneficial to have such a strict standard regarding sex outside of marriage? I would answer by offering a comparison with an ordinary household item: duct tape.

Duct tape is great; it bonds things together. It is sticky and very strong. But try this with a piece of duct tape: Bond it with one object, then peel it off and try bonding it to something else. Then peal it off and try bonding it to something else again. What you will find is that each time you remove the tape, you leave a bit of the adhesive behind. By the time you use it on the fourth object, the tape no longer functions effectively because it has lost its bonding capability. The adhesive is gone, stuck to the last three objects with which it was bonded.

The implications regarding premarital sex seem quite apparent, but try teaching that to young people today. After all, if television and the movies are to be believed, *everybody* is doing it. But let me be clear: In spite of what we see in the media, not everyone is doing it. In a recent survey of the youth in our church, we found that seventy percent of our senior high school boys disapproved of premarital sex! Nationwide surveys of communities have shown that a majority of seventeen-year-olds in the public schools—not just in the churches—have not had sex! The Centers for Disease Control in their 2001 survey noted that fifty-four percent of high school teens had not had sex.[3] And in many communities the numbers are much higher.

I received a note from a thirty-eight-year-old woman who said she was still a virgin and was saving herself for the man she hoped God would bring into her life. But she wrote, "Sometimes I wonder, is there something wrong with me?" I replied, "No, there is nothing wrong with you;

it is the rest of the world that is confused. You are a remarkable woman who is pursuing God's plans for this part of your life. You have seen sexuality as Christians are meant to see it: as a discipleship issue, a place to serve God, to trust God, to pursue God's will. This is exactly what the apostle Paul was encouraging."

But how can you save yourself for your mate? This is very, very hard! Our biological and emotional drives, coupled with our own fallen nature, make this challenging indeed. Here are a few suggestions:

Do not put yourself in a situation where you know you will be tempted to compromise. That means not being alone with your date in a place where you may succumb to pressure. If you are a teen, allow your parents to hold you accountable. Parents, this is part of your job. Know where your kids are; help them in this. They may not like it, but it is your job to protect them. Find out what time the movie gets out. Know where to reach your kids. Invite them to end the evening at your home.

I have heard parents say, "Well, they're going to do it anyway. I might as well get used to the idea." No! You may have given up, but maybe they have not. Hold out high expectations—and then offer plenty of understanding if your teenagers fail.

For all singles—youth and adults—you have to decide up front that you belong to Christ and that you want to serve him in this area by abstaining from sex. Communicate that up front. One of our singles told me recently that he and his girlfriend agreed they would not have sex until they were married. Make that agreement up front.

When I was in high school, I needed a bit of help in this area. So I brought along a Bible on my dates, a five-pound

King James Version! I placed it on the front seat, not to protect me from the girls, but to protect the girls from me. It was a reminder of the promises I had made to God.

Recently I was struck by the comments of a woman who told me that, after nearly forty years of marriage, the fact that she had been a virgin when she married still has an impact on her relationship with her husband today. He is the only man she has ever been with. Far from making her feel that she is lacking experience, it has provided the two of them with a special bond. Only they two have shared this, the most intimate and personal part of their lives. She has given herself only to this one man. And that is holy, and beautiful, and in keeping with God's plan.

Pornography and Sexual Addiction

I believe that in looking at God's plan for sexuality, it is also important to address the issue of pornography. This is a tremendous concern today. According to Family Safe Media, in 2003, revenues from pornography in the United States were nearly twice the revenues of ABC, CBS, and NBC *combined*! Family Safe Media notes that in that same year there were 4.2 million pornographic websites and 372 million pornographic webpages and that 25 percent of the daily search engine requests on the Internet were seeking pornographic websites. And this is not simply a problem for those who are outside the church. Forty-seven percent of Christians note that this is a problem in their homes.[4]

I do not know how pornography affects women; I have virtually no experience talking with women who are using pornography. But I know how it affects men and boys. Pornography is sin. It places in our minds images that reflect neither reality nor what is healthy. It feeds on the dark side of our hearts. Pornographers take what was meant to be good and beautiful and turn it into something cheap and shameful.

Pornography is also addictive. It is like a drug; it produces a physiological effect, including the release of certain chemicals and a biological response that leave you craving more. But the appetite can never be satisfied. Over time, this thing that you once toyed with becomes your master. I have known professional men—physicians, lawyers, CEOs, even pastors—who were sucked into this, risking their careers, their ministries, their families, eventually even their lives, as they became enslaved to pornography. I know many people are wrestling with this today.

Recently I was working late doing research for a sermon. As I searched the Web, using my Internet search engine, among the ten matching sites for my search was what appeared, by the description, to be a pornographic website. It was late at night, and no one was around to see what I was doing. As I sat before my computer, I had to decide if I really wanted to click on this site or not. For me the decision was made a bit easier when I asked myself several questions: Will I be proud or ashamed after I have clicked on this site? Will I be willing to tell others where I have been, or will I hope they will not find out? Will I feel closer to God or farther from God when I am finished? Will I feel more authentically human, or less, after viewing this material? Will I be able to stop with just one visit, or will I find myself needing to come back again and again? When I asked these questions, the decision not to click on the website became much easier.

I avoid these websites because I know that my human nature, marred as it is by sin, would find these sites very appealing and, in the end, addictive. I know that viewing them would produce shame in me, would alienate me from God, and would harm my relationship with my wife. Would one look ruin my life? Probably not—but I could not stop at one look.

Having ministered to many men in my congregation for whom this is a problem, I have seen firsthand its destructive power. Pornography is a counterfeit sexuality that is not God's will for our lives.

Yet, once you get started, it is hard to break this habit. But you can do it. It may be that you should not use the Internet. You may have to shut down your access to it for six months. Perhaps you need to install filters on your Internet software to help you. And certainly you need to be clear in you own mind that viewing pornography is not God's will for your life.

In addition, you will need someone to hold you accountable. If you are a teenager and pornography is a problem for you, ask your parents for help. They can help you develop an accountability plan. If you are married and you struggle with this, talk to your mate. Confess to your spouse what you are doing, and tell your spouse you do not want to do it anymore. If your spouse loves you, your spouse will want to help you. This is an addiction. You have been wounded, though you may not realize it. Your spouse can help. Allow your mate to hold you accountable.

But you may need more support than this. You may require the prayers and support of your pastor or a trained counselor. Finally, but most importantly, enlist God's help. Pornography can gain a terrible hold on you—but you can be free.

Let's return to our Scripture passage for a moment. Read the words of Paul:

[Let] each one of you know how to control your own body in holiness and honor, not with lustful passion, like the Gentiles who do not know God; that no one wrong or exploit a brother or sister in this matter, because the Lord is an avenger in all these things, just as we have already told you beforehand and solemnly warned you. For God did not call us to impurity but in holiness. (1 Thessalonians 4:4-7)

Receiving Grace and Beginning Again

I have been describing God's plan for sexual intimacy and the struggles we have in pursuing that plan. I have tried to lay out some of God's wishes for you and to give you concrete suggestions for achieving those wishes. But this discussion would not be complete if I did not offer you one last word, a word of grace.

Years ago, when I preached on this theme, a young girl came to see me who had had sex outside of marriage. With tears in her eyes she said, "Pastor Adam, I want God to forgive me. I want to be like new duct tape. I want this part of my life to be special when I marry. I wish I could go back and be a virgin again." My answer to her was simple, reflecting the very essence of the Christian faith: You can begin again. Jesus came to save us from our sin. He came to change us from the inside. He gave us his Holy Spirit to strengthen and empower us to live for him. And, yes, he is even able to make us "sticky" all over again.

Perhaps right now you would like to ask Jesus Christ for his grace, to forgive you for the secrets you have kept and for the ways you have fallen short of his plan for you.

Maybe this is the day you want to make a new commitment to him, to lay aside your sins and start over again. It is as easy as talking to him, asking his forgiveness, telling him of your desire to let go of these things, and then beginning again.

God's gift of sexual intimacy is available to you no matter how far you have strayed. Do not be confused by what the world says. Trust in Jesus. He will provide the love and support you need to bring back the beauty and joy of genuine sexual intimacy. And when you discover and live God's plans for sexual intimacy, you find one of the keys to making love last a lifetime.

---

[1] From *Marriage and Virginity,* translated by Ray Kearney, as part of *The Works of Saint Augustine: A Translation for the 21st Century* (New City Press, 1999); page 35.
[2] From www.ashastd.org/stdfaqs/statistics.html
[3] From http://www.thebody.com/siecus/adolescent_sexuality.html#what
[4] From www.familysafemedia.com/pornography_statistics.html

Personal Reflection

Individuals
- Read Leviticus 18; see also Leviticus 20. What timeless principles do you see behind these laws intended for ancient Israel?
- Read 1 Thessalonians 4:1-8. What does this teach us about sex? How does this relate to your life? What is the relationship between our spiritual life and our sex life?
- Read 1 Corinthians 6:12-20. What are the implications of this passage for you? If you are struggling with sexual addiction, talk with a pastor or Christian counselor.
- Read Luke 7:36-50. Describe the heart of Jesus in this passage. What are the implications of this passage for your life?

Couples
- Read 1 Corinthians 7:1-7, Galatians 5:22-23, and 1 John 3:16-18. How is sex an opportunity for living the gospel toward each other? Talk and pray with your spouse about how you can better minister to each other in the area of emotional and physical intimacy.

CHAPTER **7**

The Ministry and Meaning
of Faithfulness

*For everything created by God is good, and nothing is to be
rejected, provided it is received with thanksgiving; for it is
sanctified by God's word and by prayer.*

(1 Timothy 4:4-5)

*Let marriage be held in honor by all, and let the marriage
bed be kept undefiled.*

(Hebrews 13:4a)

Looking over the magazine rack at a local bookstore,
I am struck by the amount of time men and women appar-
ently spend thinking about sexual intimacy. Even more
apparent is the fact that most of us are looking for ways to
improve this part of our relationships with our mates.
Headlines scream that this magazine or that will offer "Ten
Ways to Improve Your Sex Life" or "Ten Secrets That Will
Drive Him Mad."

But popular magazines are not the only indication that
men and women sometimes have a difficult time with
physical intimacy. The 2,500 persons in my congregation

who returned surveys on this topic had a lot to say about it as well. We asked those who were married—over 1,500 persons—these two questions: "How would you characterize your physical, intimate relationship with your mate?" and "How important is the physical/sexual part of your relationship?" The answers pointed clearly to differences between men and women and helped us see that this is a very important and serious part of the marriage equation.

In this chapter my aim is to examine three things: First, I will briefly review what I laid out in the last chapter concerning God's perspective on sexual intimacy. Second, I will look at the issue of marital infidelity. And finally, I will seek to uncover biblical and theological principles that might help you discover the blessings that God intended sexual intimacy to provide within the context of marriage.

God's Perspective on Sexual Intimacy

In the previous chapter we learned that God created us as sexual beings. This was a gift from God and was meant to be a blessing in our lives. This is precisely what Paul was saying to Timothy when he wrote, "For everything created by God is good, and nothing is to be rejected, provided it is received with thanksgiving; for it is sanctified by God's word and by prayer" (1 Timothy 4:4-5). We will come back to this passage later, but for now it is important to note that God considers this part of our lives to be inherently good.

I mention this principle again because so many people, especially women and newlyweds, indicated in our surveys a certain amount of guilt associated with sexual intimacy. It can take years to overcome feelings fostered by a home or church environment that taught that sex was something to be ashamed of. That attitude, however widespread, is not supported by what we find in the Bible. For example, Professor Elizabeth Achtemeir, in her book *The Committed Marriage,* points out the interesting way that Sarah, the great matriarch of Israel, refers to sexual intimacy. In Genesis 18:12 we read, "So Sarah laughed to herself, saying, 'After I have grown old, and my husband is old, shall I have pleasure?'" Professor Achtemeir points out that the Hebrew word for pleasure is the same word used for paradise. Sarah refers to sexual intimacy as "pleasure" or "paradise."

God intended that sexual intimacy, besides bringing us pleasure, would deepen our love, creating a deep emotional bond between a woman and a man. After hearing me preach about this, one woman wrote to say that she finally understood what had happened in her past relationships with men. She said she had been intimate with several men she had dated, and each time she found that her expectations for the relationship began to escalate. She found herself bonding to the men in ways that were not always reciprocated. Learning that these emotional bonds were designed by God, she realized why she had been having that response and why God's plan is that we not become sexually intimate except within the covenant of marriage.

God intended sexual intimacy to bring pleasure and to bond us with our mates, but often it has the opposite effect. Our intimate lives can be a source of conflict, frustration, irritation, or even separation. My counseling experience over the last fifteen years indicates that nearly every couple experiences this type of stress at one time or another. Our congregational surveys painted a vivid picture of men and women who sometimes became frustrated in this area of their lives—often for very different reasons. The result was that, for them, sexual intimacy was not functioning as God intended.

At the end of this chapter I will offer one biblical perspective on sexual intimacy in marriage that could help you if you have ever struggled in this area. But first let's take a look at the struggles we face in remaining faithful in marriage.

Our Struggle With Faithfulness in Marriage

In the wedding ceremony I ask each groom this question: "Will you love her, comfort her, honor and keep her in sickness and in health, *and forsaking all others be faithful to her alone as long as you both shall live?*" I ask the same question of the bride. Faithfulness is a crucial part of the marriage vows. It has a host of meanings, but the one we will address in this chapter specifically relates to our intimate relationships. In those vows we are promising to bond only with the person we are marrying for the rest of our days.

When we are unfaithful to our mates, we commit the sin of adultery. Adultery made it to God's "Top 10 List" for ancient Israel, appearing in the seventh commandment. It was considered such a serious breach of community, such a detriment to the health of the society, that the penalty for both parties was death.

When Jesus made his sweeping statements of prohibition against divorce, he made an exception in the case of adultery. (In that circumstance he did not require divorce, but he did allow it.) Adultery was a serious enough breach of the marriage covenant that Jesus said divorce could be justified under these circumstances.

Despite societal and biblical prohibitions against infidelity, most of us will be tempted to commit this sin at some time during our married lives. The number of people who succumb to this temptation is difficult to pinpoint, however. National surveys have shown differing results. Among the published figures are those found in a poll conducted by the National Opinion Research Institute at the University of Chicago in 1992 and published in the book *Sex in America*. In that poll, fewer than twenty percent of married women and twenty-to-thirty-five percent of married men indicated they had had an extramarital affair.[1] Yet even these fairly conservative numbers indicate one in five women and as many as one in three men have been unfaithful. I would speculate that the numbers are lower for deeply committed Christians. But my experience in ministry tells me that even they can be tempted to step across the line at times.

The Anatomy of an Affair

In preparing to write this book, I sat down with a friend and asked if he would share his experience related to an affair he had told me about. He said, "It all began with a look across a room. There was an energy there. I fell in love with her, if you could call it that, during a hug. It all seemed very innocent, and yet it was very alluring. We were both married. And we were both empty. We were two needy people who were drawn to each other."

My friend went on to say that he began to feel cherished by her, just by the way she looked at him. He said her adoration was intoxicating, especially in contrast to the feelings and behavior of his wife, whose admiration for him had waned. "My wife was demanding. This woman was gentle. My wife had become critical, but this woman was constantly building me up." He fantasized about the woman for some time. Then one day she admitted her feelings for him, and the die was cast. For my friend, there was no turning back.

He told me that the physical act was not nearly as exciting as the fantasy. But immediately he and the woman began to scheme and dream about what they would do, about leaving their mates, about the life they could share. There was no sense of reality to this; he would have lost everything if he had followed through. Looking back on the affair, he said he felt he was not relating to the woman herself but only to the fantasy he had developed. After three months they broke off the relationship when their affair was discovered. My friend said, "It was like I woke up from a dream and realized how stupid I had been. What was I thinking? And I immediately separated from her."

I share this man's story because it is similar to a dozen others I have heard. This man, who had committed his life to Christ, took several wrong turns. What frightened me about his story was how easily I identified with him. Most of us will experience moments of fleeting attraction for another. There will be times we feel a "chemistry" with someone who is not our mate. I am convinced that all of us—put in the wrong set of circumstances; finding ourselves at some weak point in our lives; and forgetting our Lord, our wedding vows, and what it means to be faithful—could, with a look and a hug, begin going down a path that destroys. And it does destroy. It obliterates trust, tears families apart, wounds those with whom we have sinned, and tears at our souls. It creates a wound that is difficult to heal—difficult, but not impossible.

I have known many people whose marriages did not survive an affair. But there are just as many, including my friend, whose marriages did survive. It is important to know that there is hope, even after an affair.

I am confident that the story in the eighth chapter of the Gospel of John was included there, in part, to teach us this point. The story is that of a woman caught in the very act of adultery. The cowardly man flees, but the woman is taken before the townspeople by the religious leaders. Citing the Law of Moses, the leaders confront Jesus; and in their hands are stones with which to execute her. These people are ready to kill the woman, making no provision for grace or mercy or a bad decision or her human weakness. There is no interest in hearing that for years her husband treated her with disdain or that she had felt empty until the day the man with whom she had the affair paid attention to her. No, these people just want her dead. Jesus turns to them; and with those disarming words that still echo through history, he says, "Let anyone among you who is without sin be the first to throw a stone at her." And one by one they drop their stones and walk away. Then Jesus looks at this woman with compassion and says,

"Neither do I condemn you. Go your way, and from now on do not sin again."

Is there hope for those of you who have committed adultery? Is there hope for those of you who, like my friend, have been blinded and have been living in a fantasy? Is there hope for those of you who are hurting yourself and others by your behavior? Yes, in Jesus Christ. The way you have been living is not God's will for you. God loves you and is willing to wash you clean and make you new. But it is up to you to remember the vows you made—not only to your mate, but to God—when you promised to be faithful. Christ challenges you today to bring your affair to an end, to do whatever you must to extract yourself from it. That may involve confessing to your mate. That may involve quitting your job. That may involve moving to a new home. Be assured that God will be with you as you make these changes, empowering you to lead a new life.

Perhaps you will visit with a pastor about this and solicit help. If you are seeking to recover from an affair, you may also wish to read a helpful book entitled *Torn Asunder: Recovering From Extramarital Affairs,* by Dave Carder and others (Moody Publishers, 1995).

Affair-proofing Your Marriage

I would like to suggest some ideas that might help you to avoid an affair. The first is simply to be clear in your own mind that adultery is not God's will. Your marriage may not be happy. It may need serious help. It may not survive. But it is never God's will that you enter into an emotional or sexual relationship with another when you are married.

Next, realize that violating your marriage vows, or some-one else's, is not a foundation for a relationship that God will bless. (There are some relationships that began this way, which God later, through mercy, blessed; but these are extremely rare exceptions. The relationship between David and Bathsheba in the Bible is among these.)

Recognize your feelings when you first start to have them. Be honest about them. All of us will feel attracted toward someone who is not our spouse; I have, and I am guessing each of you has had such feelings. This is normal. The question is, What will you do with these feelings? Will you dismiss them? Or will you secretly savor them, mull them over, and fantasize about them? Walter Wangerin, in his excellent book *As for Me and My House,* describes temp-tation as "the moment of maybe." We have a choice about what we will do with our temptation; if we decide to fantasize about committing adultery, there is the likelihood that the fantasy will eventually lead to devastation.

In James 1:14-15 we read, "But one is tempted by one's own desire, being lured and enticed by it; then, when that desire has conceived, it gives birth to sin, and that sin, when it is fully grown, gives birth to death." You are the one who will decide what to do with temptation. Will you play with the idea of adultery? Will you try to move closer to the person and make yourself available to her or him? Or will you recognize the warnings and choose to remove yourself from a dangerous situation, praying that God will take away the desire?

Understand that when people's needs are not being met in their marriages, they are most susceptible to participat-ing in an affair. Do you understand the needs of your mate, and are you seeking to help meet them? When your mate feels loved by you and when your mate's emotional and sexual needs are being met, the likelihood of your mate becoming involved in an affair is greatly diminished.

Invite your spouse to help you identify potential threats to your marriage and to hold you accountable. Share your concerns, and listen to your spouse's concerns. Occasionally my wife, LaVon, expresses concern about the way a particular woman has been acting toward me. LaVon is not prone to jealousy; so when she offers such words of warning, I listen. After all, she understands far better than I do how a woman thinks. Likewise, I am aware of how men think and would likely notice a man's unhealthy interest in her.

Finally, be smart in your relationships. Do not spend extended periods of time alone with someone of the opposite sex who is not your mate. Do not share intimate stories outside of marriage. If you are having marital problems, do not discuss them with members of the opposite sex. Sharing such intimate thoughts and feelings is a dangerous first step toward an affair. And whatever you do, if you are attracted to someone outside of marriage, do not express your feelings to that person; nothing good can come of it. Think about it. If the person is not interested, you will be embarrassed and possibly lose a friend; if the person reciprocates, you will be headed down the road to an affair.

You will be the rare exception if you never experience feelings of attraction for someone who is not your mate. These feelings can be euphoric, especially if they are mutual. But while the feelings may be normal, they can have devastating consequences when acted upon. They can destroy your family, your mate, your career, and your future. Worse, they can separate you from God.

So, when temptation comes your way, remember your calling in marriage, allow your mate to help you, and do not believe the devil's lies that such thoughts are harmless. Guard your heart.

A Roller Coaster

In some ways, sexual intimacy in marriage is like a roller coaster. Sexual intimacy is seldom like it is portrayed in the movies, especially for newlyweds, for whom sex can be awkward and frustrating. This is particularly true if they have not been sexually active before marriage. There is a wonderful blessing and joy in learning how to be intimate together, however. It means that the sexual relationship in marriage will be like a fine wine that improves with age!

For many couples, just as things are starting to improve in this area, there is a new development: children. When we looked at the results of our congregational survey, we found an interesting contrast. More than fifty percent of all married men in their twenties, forties, fifties, and older said that their intimate relationships were excellent or very good (with a high in the sixty percent range for those in their sixties); while for married men in their thirties the number was just thirty percent. Consistently this difference was attributed to having children and the time and energy that go into caring for them. Parents often are exhausted from taking care of the house and the kids, to say nothing of holding down a job. They frequently have no energy, no emotional strength, and no passion left at the end of the day.

Parents, listen carefully: *This is normal. And it is not permanent.* Things will get better, as evidenced in our survey by the marked increase in married men's sexual satisfaction as time goes by. In the meantime, couples with small children need to plan weekends away from the kids; and parents would do well to give each other a break from the kids on a regular basis.

When you finally do get to spend some time together, talk to each other and actively seek to meet each other's needs. One husband recently told me that after more than two decades of marriage, he had learned something new about sexual intimacy. He learned that if he spent twenty minutes simply rubbing his wife's back and feet, touching her and massaging her, seeking to bring pleasure to her, she nearly always responded to his sexual advances in positive ways. The key, he noted, was the earnestness with which he genuinely sought to bless her by his touch, rather than simply trying to "get her in the mood."

Sexual Intimacy as Ministry and Agape

In this study we have learned that many women long for intimacy in conversation, romance, and affectionate touch. We also learned that many men have a strong need for sexual touch. God created men and women to be helpers in meeting one another's needs. Finally, we learned that God intended sexual intimacy to be a means of bonding husband and wife together. I now want to offer a biblical and theological idea that could make a tremendous difference in this part of your life.

Paul writes,

The husband should give to his wife her conjugal rights, and likewise the wife to her husband. For the wife does not have authority over her own body, but the husband does; likewise the husband does not have authority over his own body, but the wife does. Do not deprive one another except perhaps by agreement for a set time, to devote yourselves to prayer, and then come together again. (1 Corinthians 7:3-5)

Paul is telling us that when a man marries, his body no longer belongs to him; it belongs to his wife. And Paul is telling us that when a woman marries, her body no longer belongs to her; it belongs to her husband. Husband and wife are to minister to each other through the act of physical intimacy.

Consider this: As Christians we are called to care for one another, to demonstrate the special kind of love we learned about earlier, called "agape." Agape is about giving, not receiving. It does not look for what it will receive in return; it looks for what it can give in order to bless. It is on this understanding of love that a satisfying intimate relationship can be built, not on reading about the latest techniques or purchasing the most exotic lingerie.

When we see affectionate touch, romance, and sexual intimacy as opportunities for ministry rather than as duties, then something wonderful takes place: These acts become holy. It is in such spiritual acts of self-giving, when we open ourselves to our mates and devote ourselves completely to caring for them in the most vulnerable, beautiful, and personal way possible, that we begin to discover the deeper meaning of physical intimacy.

The authors of the book *Sex in America* discovered in their survey that deeply committed Christians actually had a higher quality of intimate relationship than non-

Christians.[2] The authors may have been surprised, but I was not. When two people receive sexual intimacy as a gift from God, when they guard their hearts, when they see marriage as a sacred calling and sex as a means of self-giving, they are likely to discover the quality of sexual intimacy God intended for us to have all along. For them, sex is holy, beautiful, passionate. It is the living, physical embodiment of agape.

---

[1] From *Sex in America: A Definitive Survey,* by John H. Gagnon, Edward O. Laumann, and Gina Kolata (Little, Brown and Company, 1994, 1995); page 105.
[2] From *Sex in America: A Definitive Survey;* pages 127, 130.

Personal Reflection

Individuals
- Read Exodus 20:14. Why do you think avoiding this sin was among the foundational commands God gave to Israel? Now read Proverbs 6:23-35, 1 Corinthians 7:2-5, and Hebrews 13:4. Why is adultery warned against in these passages? What effect does adultery have on all parties involved?
- Read Matthew 5:27-30. What is Jesus' point? Are you ever tempted in this way? What can you do to guard against opening the door to an inappropriate relationship?
- Read John 8:1-11. What do we learn about the heart of Jesus from this passage? God is able to forgive us and restore us. Does this mean that all marriages can survive adultery? Why or why not? How is a marriage able to survive adultery?

Couples
- Women need affection, romance, and caring words and touch. Men have a strong need for sexual intimacy. Discuss how you can intentionally meet each other's needs while creating an intimate relationship that regularly involves both. How can you minister to your spouse in the way she or he receives intimacy?
- Discuss specific ways you can help each other to guard against infidelity and remain faithful to each other.
- Share your thoughts with each other regarding John 8:1-11 and the related questions above. If you are dealing with adultery, talk with a pastor or trusted Christian counselor.

CHAPTER 8

Making Love Last a Lifetime

Two are better than one, because they have a good reward for their toil. For if they fall, one will lift up the other; but woe to one who is alone and falls and does not have another to help. Again, if two lie together, they keep warm; but how can one keep warm alone? And though one might prevail against another, two will withstand one. A threefold cord is not quickly broken.

(Ecclesiastes 4:9-12)

We have looked at love, marriage, and sex from many different perspectives, all with one objective in mind: making love last a lifetime. Lasting love is the dream of every bride and groom on their wedding day, as well as the hope of many singles as they search for that perfect mate. They want a partner for life, for good and bad times, someone with whom they can share goals and dreams. God shares these dreams.

We have seen, however, that making love last a lifetime is not an easy task. Life gets in the way. Human nature sets in. Money problems may put a strain on the relationship.

Both spouses may be so busy earning a living that they have little time for each other. They grow apart. Some find they can live together in marriage without love, and some do that. Others separate or divorce. A fortunate few find a way to make love last a lifetime, as God intended in creating love, marriage, and sex. And you can, too.

A strong relationship with Jesus Christ is the foundation of a healthy marriage. If you have read this far, you should not find that statement surprising. Our marriages need a partnership with God in order to thrive and to last. And God wants to be a part of our marital lives. That is what we are going to examine in this final chapter: the connection between a relationship with God and a long, happy marriage. But first, a word to singles.

Being Christian and Single

Being a Christian single can be both a gift and a blessing. You may be looking for a life partner, but I encourage you not to make the search for a mate the primary focus of your life. If you want to be married, let God know the desire of your heart. Pray and lay this desire at Jesus' feet. But do not allow this to be your one consuming desire. If you do, you will miss out on the life God has already given you.

The apostle Paul speaks to singles in 1 Corinthians 7:8, 32-34:

> To the unmarried.... I say that it is well for them to remain unmarried.... I want you to be free from anxieties. The unmarried man [or woman] is anxious about the affairs of the Lord ... but [those who are married are] anxious about the affairs of the

world, how to please [their spouses], and [their] interests are divided.

I do not believe Paul means that you should avoid marriage but that you are in a unique position right now to have undivided loyalties and unwavering focus. You can pursue Christian faith and ministry in a way that married people cannot. Some have described this situation as being "radically available" to God.

At the same time, your need for companionship is still present as a single. You need friends, companions, helpers; and that is where Christian community comes in. Are you active in a group with other singles? If not, I encourage you to consider joining such a group, not just as a place where you can look for a potential mate, but where you can grow in your faith; build friendships based upon shared values; and find others to help, encourage, and stand by you as you serve the Lord.

Many churches offer activities for singles that provide spiritual growth and meet the needs of various age groups. Bible studies, Sunday school classes, fellowship events, and mission trips are just some of the settings in which you can develop strong bonds of friendship that can last a lifetime. You can be a blessing to others while participating in a singles group. As a single you can help achieve God's purposes. You are of great value to God.

God's Plan for Christian Marriage

Among the basic premises of the Christian life is that every part of our lives represents a place and opportunity in which to serve God. We do not serve God just on

Sundays. Every day, every moment, we are called to serve the Lord.

To that end I have encouraged you to see marriage in a new light. Marriage is not falling head over heels in love; it is not simply a relationship between two people who cannot stand to be apart. Marriage is a part of God's plan. It is a calling, a mission in which two people enter into a covenant with God to minister to each other.

If you choose to be married, the marriage covenant becomes a part of God's plan for your life. Your spouse becomes the one person above all others whom God calls you to minister to, to bless, to encourage. Surprising as it may sound, marriage is not primarily an act of love; it is primarily an act of discipleship, faithfulness, service, and obedience to God. When seen in this way, marriage takes on a new meaning and offers us the possibility of remarkable joy and satisfaction.

Much of the data on what makes for a fulfilling marriage shows that one of the key ingredients is a sense of shared purpose or meaning between the spouses. In *The Seven Principles for Making Marriage Work,* John Gottman notes that one of the principles for making marriage work is the creation of shared meaning between husband and wife.[1]

Unfortunately, many people invest that sense of shared meaning or purpose in things that do not last. These people share a common goal of becoming wealthy, or a sense of purpose in rearing their children, or a commitment to certain kinds of civic service. But wealth, once achieved, offers little basis for shared meaning. Children grow up and move away. Even civic service, while important and noble, can become so much busy work when pursued as an end in itself. But those of us who are Christians have something more: a calling to serve God together, every day and in every part of our lives.

Those of us who enter into *Christian* marriage share a calling to serve God together. We marry because as husband and wife, we can accomplish more in service to God together than either of us can accomplish alone. Christian marriage is not a calling simply to serve each other; it is a calling to serve God and others as well.

As you know by now, my wife, LaVon, and I married when we were quite young. We have changed over the years; we are not the same people we were in 1982 when we married. Truly, we were just children then. We would have grown apart; and I am convinced that we would not be married today were it not for the fact that we share a common foundation, a common sense of meaning, and a common purpose for our lives.

LaVon's aim is to serve Christ. Her desire is to know him, to pursue his will, to serve God in every area of her life, including in our marriage. My aim is to serve Christ. It is to know him, to pursue his will, to serve God in every area of my life, including in our marriage. This is our shared vision for our lives. We want it to be our consuming passion. As a result, the closer we get to Christ, the nearer we draw to each other. Over the last twenty years I have found that I am always most in love with LaVon when I feel closest to God. This is both the secret and the joy of Christian marriage.

When Your Mate Is Not a Christian

I have told my daughters that if they date someone who is not a Christian, they may fall in love with someone who is not a Christian; and consequently they may find themselves marrying someone who is not a Christian. Because of this, one of the most critical things to look for in a mate—even in a date—is Christian faith.

The person you are dating may have everything; this person may be kind, physically attractive, stable, secure, and a great conversationalist. But, as wonderful as these qualities are, somewhere down the road you are going to want more; you will want and need someone with whom you can share your faith, your soul, your values, and your life purpose. Please take this issue seriously. If you are dating someone who is not a believer, tell him or her how important your faith is to you and invite this person to join you in going to church. Read this book together, and take the time to discuss it.

But what if you already are in a marriage in which your spouse is not a Christian? I receive many notes and letters from those whose mates are not people of faith. In most cases the greatest desire of the persons who write these notes is that their mates come to share the joy they have found in Christ. They want their mates to attend church with them, to pray with them, to follow Christ with them.

I would remind you of the apostle Paul's words in 1 Corinthians 7:12-14:

> If any believer has a wife who is an unbeliever, and she consents to live with him, he should not divorce her. And if any woman has a husband who is an unbeliever, and he consents to live with her, she should not divorce him. For the unbelieving husband is made holy through his wife, and the unbelieving wife is made holy through her husband.

I am not certain what Paul had in mind, but I think he might have meant that over time we rub off on our mates. Over time the Holy Spirit shines through us to them.

But this requires an extraordinary measure of grace and patience. You cannot focus on what your mate is not; this will only drive a wedge between you, a wedge that you created. You can, however, look at your mate through the eyes of Christ. You can gently bear witness to your faith using words that do not cast judgment but instead communicate how important your faith is to you. You can pray for your mate. And you can demonstrate the love of Christ to your mate in tangible ways.

One woman in my congregation said that she gives herself to her husband through physical intimacy with a greater passion now than before she became a Christian as she seeks to help him see Christ in her and let him know that such passion comes from her faith. Another woman wrote me this note:

> My marriage is good because I continue to fall deeper in love with Jesus. I never miss my daily appointment with him. And he just keeps me focused on changes he wants to make in me, keeps my eyes focused on *my* faults, keeps my heart grateful for all of my blessings.

I would offer one word to any spouses who are not Christians and who may be reading this book. One way to bless your mate is to attend church with him or her, even if you are not a believer. That one hour per week, as a demonstration of respect for and partnership with your spouse, can do amazing things to help your mate know of your love and care and in the process will strengthen your marriage. In my congregation I have persons who are atheists and agnostics as well as persons who are members of other religions. These people attend worship with their spouses as a way of expressing love for them. Even if you are not a Christian, if your mate is serious about his or her faith, you would do well to share in and be supportive of it. In doing so, you may find your marriage strengthened and your life enriched.

The Importance of Faith, Prayer, and a Church Family

One of the reasons I have written this book is because I hope that some who are not yet Christians, or are nominally Christian, might come to see that Christianity has much to offer in the areas of love, marriage, and sex. God has a plan for each of these important areas of our lives. When we stray from God's plans, we sometimes find pain. When we pursue God's plans, we find a quality of marriage we never dreamed possible.

Both for the nominally religious who are reading this book and those of you who are Christians, my hope is that you might have a Christian marriage, a marriage in which Jesus Christ is both the foundation and the destination. It is in growing deeper in your faith, in praying for your mate, in falling in love with Christ, and in seeing the difference he can make in your relationships that you will find not only your marriage but also your entire life enriched. This kind of faith changes everything.

There are several thousand married couples in my church who have only recently become Christians. One such couple, who had not been a part of a church since they were small children, came to me after worship not long ago. They told me that they had always had a pretty solid marriage; but since coming to the church and committing their lives to Christ, their marriage had gone to a whole new level. They had found a joy, a love, and a quality of life they had never known before.

There is a joy and purpose, a partnership and love, that cannot be fully experienced apart from a relationship with God. This is how I read this enigmatic and interesting passage from Ecclesiastes 4:9-12:

> Two are better than one, because they have a good reward for their toil. For if they fall, one will lift up the other; but woe to one who is alone and falls and does not have another to help. Again, if two lie together, they keep warm; but how can one keep warm alone? And though one might prevail against another, two will withstand one. A threefold cord is not quickly broken.

The first few lines of this passage make sense—"Two are better than one." But it is the last line that people of faith find most intriguing: "A threefold cord is not quickly broken." What is the third strand the author speaks of? I believe it is God; God is the third partner who makes the marriage covenant very difficult to break.

It is that third strand that I so want you to experience. And you will, together with your mate, when you invite Christ to be a part of your life, when you see your marriage as a ministry, when you and your spouse pray with and for each other, when you become involved in a church family where you can grow in your faith and serve God. When you do these things, you will discover that love truly can last a lifetime.

---

[1] From *The Seven Principles for Making Marriage Work,* by John Gottman (Three Rivers Press, 2000); page 243.

Personal Reflection

Individuals

- According to Ecclesiastes 4:9-12, why are two better than one? To what does the "threefold cord" refer? How does Christ strengthen a relationship?
- Ask God to supply your needs and equip you to follow through.
- Read John 13:1-17. What does Jesus teach us? How is God calling you to serve those closest to you—especially the man or woman you love? Ask God to give you the humble, willing heart of a servant.
- Singles: Read 1 Corinthians 7:14. What are Paul's major points? Verse 17 of 1 Corinthians 7 in *The Message* says, "God, not your marital status, defines your life." What implications does this have for your life?
- Singles: Read 2 Corinthians 6:14. Do you think this passage contradicts 1 Corinthians 7:14 in any way? Why or why not? Why is it advisable not to marry someone who does not share your faith in Christ?

Couples

- Ask, "What can I do to encourage you?" Commit to your spouse for and encourage each other in these areas.
- Share your reflections on John 13:1-17—and, as you are led, the ways God is calling you to serve each other. Take turns washing each other's feet. Let this be a reverent, sacred act expressing your desire to serve God by serving each other. End with a word of prayer together.